CULTURE
TO
THE MAX!

CULTURE
TO MAX!
THE

CULTURALLY RESPONSIVE TEACHING AND PRACTICE

DAVID McDONALD, M.ED.

DANIELLE ROSS, M.ED.

ANDRE ROSS, M.ED.

SHONTORIA WALKER, ED.D.

ILLUSTRATED BY CAMERON WILSON

JB JOSSEY-BASS™
A Wiley Brand

Jossey-Bass
A Wiley Imprint
111 River St, Hoboken, NJ 07030
www.josseybass.com

Jossey-Bass books and products are available through most bookstores. To contact Jossey-Bass directly, call our Customer Care Department within the U.S. at 800–956–7739, outside the U.S. at +1-317-572-3986, or fax +1-317-572-4002.

Wiley also publishes its books in a variety of electronic formats and by print-on-demand. Some material included with standard print versions of this book may not be included in e-books or in print-on-demand. If this book refers to media such as a CD or DVD that is not included in the version you purchased, you may download this material at **http://booksupport.wiley.com**. For more information about Wiley products, visit **www.wiley.com**.

Library of Congress Cataloging-in-Publication Data

Names: McDonald, David (Educator), author. | Ross, Danielle (Educator),
   author. | Ross, Andre (Educator), author. | Walker, Shontoria, author.
Title: Culture to the max! : culturally responsive teaching and practice /
   David McDonald, Danielle Ross, Andre Ross, Shontoria Walker.
Description: Hoboken, NJ : Jossey-Bass, [2022] | Includes index.
Identifiers: LCCN 2022010312 (print) | LCCN 2022010313 (ebook) | ISBN
   9781119832416 (paperback) | ISBN 9781119832430 (adobe pdf) | ISBN
   9781119832423 (epub)
Subjects: LCSH: Multicultural education. | Culturally relevant pedagogy. |
   Educational equalization.
Classification: LCC LC1099 .M42 2022 (print) | LCC LC1099 (ebook) | DDC
   370.117—dc23/eng/20220511
LC record available at https://lccn.loc.gov/2022010312
LC ebook record available at https://lccn.loc.gov/2022010313

COVER DESIGN: PAUL MCCARTHY
COVER ART: © GETTY IMAGES | KLAUS VEDFELT

FIRST EDITION
SKY10034027_061422

*We dedicate this
book to the students who
sat in our classrooms. There
would be no us, without you.
To our families and mentors,
who were our first teachers
and showed us what responsive
teaching looked like before we
even knew what it was.*

CONTENTS

CULTURE
TO
THE MAX!

INTRODUCTION

Not everything that is faced can be changed, but nothing can be changed until it is faced.

—James Baldwin

Students of color are not broken. The educational system designed to serve them, is. Educators have often heard of the vast opportunity gaps between students of color. However, the deep-rooted systemic problems are often absent from the conversation. Beyond the inequities in school funding. Beyond the lack of access to resources and challenging curriculum. The educational experiences of students of color are different from their white counterparts. From the moment they walk into the schoolhouse to the moment that they leave the school grounds, the experience of schooling for students of color is unparalleled. In traditional teaching styles, how students walk, talk, their lived experiences and cultural backgrounds are not considered high on the priority list of leading to academic achievement and success (Emdin, 2017). As an organization, Education PowerED is here to tell you that embedding a student's cultural background into their learning experiences is the key to their social, emotional, and academic success.

Founded in 2019, Education PowerED is one of the fastest growing movements in education promoting culturally responsive teaching (CRT) practices to transform and shift the culture of education. Based in Dallas and Houston,

Texas, Education PowerED consists of two entities, (1) Education PowerED 501(c)3, a nonprofit research organization that provides access to research-informed, transformative educational frameworks that centers originally produced teacher materials as the foundational model of our work and (2) Education PowerED Consulting Agency, where we facilitate professional development trainings named the *Educator Empowerment Series*, using culturally responsive classroom lessons, tools, and resources. Over 20,000+ educators engage with our brand daily. The professional development experiences that we lead are intentionally designed to equip educators with the mindset and knowledge necessary to implement CRT into their classrooms.

The disparities in student experiences have been documented long past landmark policy laws that shifted education, such as *Brown vs. Board of Education*. The U.S. Supreme Court ruled segregated schools unconstitutional in 1954. According to archived studies, extensive research includes first-hand accounts of how integration altered the schooling experiences of students of color. For example, stories like Ms. Ruby Sales, who became the director and founder of the nonprofit organization Spirit House and served as a former member of the Student Nonviolent Coordinating Committee (SNCC), challenged that many people fail to look to the past to seek answers to our current problems in education. She commanded that America is dealing with a "counterculture" of education after segregation was ruled unconstitutional, which would enable students of color not to be the victims of the current educational system. Sales documented how Southern Black teachers who shared the same hue as most of their students before segregation were phenomenal educational leaders and students of their craft, while many still exist today. However, no one has been compelled to ask those educators how they managed to do it? What tools and skills did they use to vitalize students to believe that they could impact the world around them even when society says they couldn't? What critical instructional strategies might we learn from them? How may they deal with complicated student-teacher interactions when an understanding of self is misaligned?

Other critical stories from trailblazers such as Ms. Julia Matilda Burns detailed her experiences of how identity and culture were stripped away from students of color as they integrated white spaces. She noted that her white counterparts had gone the extra mile to preserve their students' identity by continuing to recreate their own sacred spaces in the form of private institutions with high tuition costs even after integration. From the broader view, these private institutions offered specialized training by highly qualified educators, accelerated academic tracks, guaranteed college-bound pathways to Ivy League institutions, and promises of producing well-rounded students with unique extracurricular programs. It sounded like the perfect institution for all students to excel. However, students of color were not welcomed in these spaces. As integration became the law of the land and Black students integrated white schools and majority white communities, white families would move to protect and preserve who they were in what is deemed as white flight. Therefore, the schools that were meant to provide better opportunities for all students became a beacon of growing opportunity gaps between students of color and their white peers.

As a school board member, educator, and parent in Holmes County, Mississippi, Ms. Burns noted that when her Black son and his peers attempted to integrate a white school in Tchula in 1965, the school was burned down twice. As a plan to bypass the new integration laws in the South, the local white community chose to start their private white academy to maintain their status quo. While her son continued to attend the newly integrated schools, they were treated as less than undeserving, and although they were children, they felt as though they were seen as adults and thus treated as adults in school settings. Additionally, she documented her own schooling experiences, like the first time she ever saw a brand-new textbook in her freshman year of high school due to a new course requirement to graduate.

In addition to the tumultuous experience of schooling for Black students during integration, LatinX students experienced similar resistance approximately ten years prior, which set a precedent to the *Brown vs. Board of Education* decision. In 1944, a Mexican American parent named Gonzalo Méndez was told by the Orange County School District that his three children had to attend the Mexican school even though their fair skin cousins attended the white school in the district. Though no laws legally allowed segregation for LatinX families and children, Méndez and other Mexican American families sued the district. They won the class-action lawsuit in the *Méndez vs. Westminster* trial and at appellate levels of the federal court system. Young Sylvia Méndez recalled hearing the white defendants cite evidence stating that due to lack of exposure to segregation, Spanish-speaking children were developmentally disabled in learning the English language and blending races within white schools developed a typical cultural attitude against the American ideals. Though the Mexican schools, as Méndez recalled, lacked the proper resources to build academic knowledge and skills with half-torn, second-hand textbooks and wooden shacks, and instead focused on preparing the young boys for labor work and the young girls for housekeeping, she would rather stay at the schools where she felt welcomed than go to a school that considered her less than.

Manuel Sandoval recalled similar experiences to Méndez's with separated educational spaces between races, Black and white, and between citizenship, American and Panamanian. When the United States included the Panama Canal Zone, he noted that he never experienced discrimination until he and his family lived in the Canal Zone, where there was a clear distinction between Black Americans, Black Panamanians, and white Americans. Because the *Brown vs. Board* decision only applied explicitly to race and not citizenship, those who belonged to Panamanian or West Indian citizenship remained segregated long after the decision. When Spanish language instruction replaced U.S.-based English instruction for non-U.S. citizens in Latin America, West-Indian children who grew up on English-speaking islands were left at a disadvantage. The cultural shift of language and education created a massive exodus of Central American immigrants to the U.S. between 1960 and 1970.

STUDENT ACHIEVEMENT

The opportunity gap of students of color has continued to widen over time. Though the new law deemed segregation unconstitutional, and schools began to integrate, highly qualified, certified, Black teachers were not welcomed in these educational institutions (Fay, 2018). Therefore, students who once felt a sense of belonging at their previous schools, with most teachers who may have looked like them, were now stripped of the significance of kinship. Where self-actualization was once a priority for students of color and the educators who served them, feelings of personal unfulfillment, personal dissatisfaction, self-alienation, and detachment from the curriculum and instruction now plagued the classroom environment. The cultural climate of the schoolhouses shifted from high expectations and accountability to survival. As we continue to place a magnifying glass on the elements of the educational system, we then begin to see how the shift to standardized testing has continued to be the avenue of these disparities in student achievement throughout history.

As the demographic makeup of American schools began to change, standardized testing initially designed to measure achievement to attain access to either military opportunities or higher levels of education, unfortunately, was found to be deeply biased towards students from communities of color, specifically from low-income communities (Bazzaz, 2017). From the Scholastic Aptitude Test (SAT) in 1926 to the American College Testing (ACT) in the 1950s to state-mandated testing, the ability to authentically assess students became a distant dream for educators who believe that if creative assessments are built based on the realistic situations of students, then the idea of success would be accessible for all, adding a layer to the student experience of schooling.

If I, as a student of color, sit for an assessment, and due to the inequity in the quality of my textbooks at my school, I cannot read at a proficient level, I am already at a loss. If I, as a student of color, open my assessment and due to a lack of funding because of my zip code and the allocated property taxes, my school cannot take me on field lessons to expand my perspective on the world, I do not have enough background knowledge to answer the questions correctly. If I, as a student of color, cannot use my cultural cues and community reference to answer the questions correctly, then I fail the assessment. If I, as a student of color, am unable to attain success on the academic achievement assessment designed to measure my knowledge and skills, then I may miss opportunities to gain better employment; to gain opportunities for a college education; to gain opportunities to advance in the workforce. Because the underlying bias in standardized testing is not addressed by those who are in positions of power, if

I fail this assessment, then I, as a student of color, may be mis-diagnosed as having a learning disability, or misplaced in spe-cial education, or required to take remedial courses because of my test score on an assessment that was not designed for me to achieve success, as a student of color, in the first place (García, 2008). Now, this never-ending cycle of my experience as a student of color sitting for a standardized assessment has transcended generations of my family and, as a result, created a history of socioeconomic disadvantage.

Studies have shown that regardless of whether the school is high performing or low performing, students of color tend to lack proficient knowledge and skills in all disciplines, most often beginning from the 4th–8th grade, where long-term suc-cess is usually predicted, debunking the myth that students of color are only under-achieving in low-scoring, poverty-stricken schools with minimal sources (Irvine, 1991). When historical failures of academic achievement become the recurring story-line of students of color, where Black, LatinX, Native American, and Native/Pacific Islander students continue to score lower than white students, where does that leave us?

WHY CULTURALLY RESPONSIVE TEACHING AND PRACTICE?

Referencing James Baldwin's quote mentioned at the beginning of this chapter, we must face the broken educational system to change it. It has become clear that disrupting the opportunity gap through funding and resources alone is not enough. While the demographic makeup of the student body has changed over time, the teacher force has remained mainly unchanged. In recent years, approximately 80% of teachers are white, while 9% are LatinX, 7% are Black, 1% are American Indian, and less than 1% are Pacific Islander. While the average teacher in an American classroom is a 43-year-old white woman, the average perception of education is from the white male-dominated perspective embedded within the school curriculum. The cultural, behavioral, and language differences are key contributing factors to the dynamic of the experiences of students of color inside and outside the classroom (Banks and McGee, 2004). Unfortunately, the attributes that make students of color unique in the educational setting are used as a source of consequence and retribution, resulting in students of color being held to lower academic expectations simply for being misunderstood. The glaring demographic differences between students and teachers magnify the need to develop more culturally responsive educators inside the classroom.

Culture can be described as a student's customary beliefs , social norms, and material traits of religious, racial or social groups. From the start of education reform, every student's cultural background should have been permanently embedded within their learning experience. It should have always been an essential determinant in the composition of standardized testing, in creating all levels of the school curriculum, designing schoolhouses, hiring school and district leaders, and educators, as well as in the adoption of education policy laws. Although we may find this instance in small subsets of educational institutions, it continues to not be enough to impact most of the student body that has a seat in our classrooms today. We have taken from education a student's way of being and existing in this world. Teachers' lack of cultural awareness, understanding of multicultural education, and equity pedagogy knowledge prevent them from recognizing personal perceptions and biases that could negatively impact student outcomes (Aguado et al., 2003). As a result, educators tend to enforce "self-selected" policy and practices, unaware that they impose learning obstructions to academic success.

Consequently, student frustration and disengagement are commonly mistaken for a disregard for education, resulting in high suspension rates, high expulsion rates, and an overall low educational attainment for students of color. Thus, the cycle continues. Students deserve an education that is relevant to who they are and responsive to whom they are becoming. Quality education requires relevance and rigor to produce positive academic and social results to improve the experiences of students of color.

CULTURALLY RESPONSIVE TEACHING DOMAINS AND STANDARDS

Culturally Responsive Teaching and Practice is a pedagogy that acknowledges the need to include a student's cultural references, including identity, language, and geographical location, in their learning. A term coined by Dr. Gloria Ladson-Billings, pedagogical theories and educator, and expounded upon by other scholars such as Dr. Geneva Gay, Zaretta Hammond, Sharroky Hollie, and many others, all have agreed that culturally responsive teaching should be the focal point for supporting students of color and improving the performance and student experience within the classroom. Culturally responsive teaching benefits all students as it encourages them to seek a deeper understanding of themselves, others, and the surrounding world while engaging in contextual learning experiences. The primary goal of culturally responsive teaching is to leverage students' strengths to make learning more representative, rigorous, impactful, and effective. To create lasting change, annual cultural heritage celebrations, checklists of instructional strategies, and race-based data reflections should not be the only way we represent culturally responsive teaching practices in educational institutions. Cultural responsiveness must be explicit and transparent if we genuinely desire to see the opportunity gap's erasure and educators on a personal quest to strengthen their practice (Ladson-Billings, 2009).

Therefore, through extensive research and to advance on the work of the pioneer scholars and researchers, Education PowerED has developed culturally responsive teaching standards and domains that can be used as a criterion and guideline to produce a sound, culturally responsive classroom. We have found that educators continue to report feeling inadequate to teach the multicultural or anti-bias curriculum (Banks, 2007). Therefore, based on our personal experiences as students of color as well as educators reared in the American education system, our solution was to develop a reference that could be used in school-wide training, district professional development, and teacher preparation programs to increase a more effective, efficient, and coherent school and classroom culture so that we do not continue to repeat the intergenerational inequity of education of experiences of the same likings as Ms. Julia Matilda Burns and her children, young Sylvia Méndez, and Manuel Sandoval.

The culturally responsive teaching domains and standards that Education PowerED has developed outline the mindsets, actions, and behaviors observed in culturally responsive classrooms. As we can look to the past as a reference in the lack of teacher preparation for students of color, this book is about the embodiment of a culturally responsive educator from four expert educators who were aware and sure of their cultural backgrounds, their own lived realities, and experiences, their own biases, and their personal, educational journeys in the hopes to add value to the ones that came before them. As we take Dr. Ladson-Billings's work a step further, we practice the implementation of cultural responsiveness and our progress of understanding of what a true culturally responsive educator means so that you, as the reader, can see the positive impact that it has made on our classrooms. To reimagine education that will transcend generations for students of color.

A culturally responsive educator means that we are collaborating in **Community and Family Partnerships** to ensure practical kinship that allows students of color to learn through contextualized experiences and multiple perspectives to enhance the learning experience.

A culturally responsive educator means that educators have **Culture Management** where they can create inclusive, positive, and productive classroom environments that eliminate cognitive barriers and create an optimal learning environment for students to engage in meaningful instruction.

A culturally responsive educator means that educators have **Authentic Engagement** that will engage students through all five different modes of learning; intellectual, emotional, physical, and behavioral that drives student motivation through rigorous learning opportunities that challenge student critical thinking.

A culturally responsive educator means that educators select **Social Justice** curriculum materials and resources that create a space within the classroom to discuss the histories of oppression, inequities, and analyze current injustices that allow students to reflect on their lived experiences, explore social issues, and become social change agents.

In this book, we honor the students that we write about. For without them, there would be no us.

EDUCATION POWERED'S CULTURALLY RESPONSIVE TEACHING DOMAINS AND STANDARDS

The Culturally Responsive Teaching Domains and Standards listed below outlines the mindsets, actions, and behaviors observed in culturally responsive classrooms. Our research process consisted of five phases that included first identifying scholars and research that provided background and context of cultural responsiveness. Next, we reviewed research to pinpoint common culturally responsive skills, mindsets, and actions necessary to be effective in the classroom. After we synthesized the skills, we used them to develop explicit standards and categorized these standards into relevant domains. Lastly, we hosted focus groups of current educators across the country to receive feedback on the effectiveness of the standards in creating a sound, culturally responsive classroom to enhance the learning experience for all students. These domains and standards are outlined below.

DOMAIN 1: COMMUNITY PARTNERSHIPS

Community Partnerships refers to the collaboration between the classroom teacher and integral members of the students' lives; mainly family and community members. Effective partnerships with community and family will result in consistent connections between the classroom and the school community. This provides students with opportunities to make sense of their learning through contextualized experiences and offers multiple perspectives to enhance their experience.

Standard	Title	"The Culturally Responsive Teacher is able to. . ."
1.1	Community Knowledge	Gain critical knowledge about the local community and students' families, including history, culture, and values. Teacher leverages community knowledge to foster a safe and responsive learning environment.
1.2	Family Involvement	Develop trusting relationships with diverse families to maintain involvement throughout the year. Teacher consistently incorporates family input and insight when determining academic goals, curriculum, and expectations.
1.3	Contextual Learning	Build bridges of meaning between the classroom and the student's home community. Teacher utilizes real-world events, issues, and information as the basis by which students explore and engage in learning.
1.4	Support Systems	Invites family and community members to be active participants in maintaining the social emotional well-being of students. Teacher facilitates opportunities for students to talk about identity, experiences, and other aspects of their lives.

Standard	Title	"The Culturally Responsive Teacher is able to. . ."
1.5	Local Partnerships	Partners with local organizations, businesses, and leaders to maximize learning experiences through guest presentations, interviews, demonstrations, etc.
1.6	Community Service	Create opportunities for students to build community through volunteerism that directly benefits the community.

DOMAIN 2: CULTURE MANAGEMENT

Culture Management refers to the teacher's ability to create a positive, inclusive, safe, and productive classroom environment for students. Effective culture management eliminates barriers and creates an optimal learning environment for students to engage with instruction and retain learning. This domain leverages brain-based theories to support the practices to foster, maintain, and rebuild classroom culture.

Standard	Title	"The Culturally Responsive Teacher is able to. . ."
2.1	High Expectations	Explicitly communicate high expectations for students academically and socially. The teacher ensures expectations are reflective of students' home culture and identity.

Standard	Title	"The Culturally Responsive Teacher is able to. . ."
2.2	Collective Responsibility	Create a community-centered learning environment where students are expected to be individually and collectively accountable for successes and failures. Teacher structures environments for cooperative learning and group activities.
2.3	Relationships	Establish meaningful interpersonal relationships with all students and foster healthy interactions between students. Teacher-student relationships extend beyond the bounds of the classroom as the teacher shows genuine interest in each student.
2.4	Authenticity	Celebrate the social, cultural, and linguistic differences among students openly and explore these differences with students. The teacher encourages students to represent themselves authentically (verbal communication, body language, cultural expressions, etc.)
2.5	Harmony	Nurture positive emotions in students that will support learning and ensure that students feel safe, cared for, and welcomed. The teacher supports students in developing a positive self-image and beliefs about others.

Standard	Title	"The Culturally Responsive Teacher is able to. . ."
2.6	Organization of Space	Establish a physically inviting classroom where decor, posters, flags, and other educational materials featured throughout the classroom reflect the cultural diversity of the students and the school community. The teacher arranges classroom space optimally for social interactions including small group discussions, presentations, movement, and teacher-student collaborative space.
2.7	Classroom Systems	Cultivates a classroom environment that reflects diversity, equity, and justice. Teacher actions apply equitably to all students while ensuring policies, procedures, and rewards do not isolate certain groups of students.
2.8	Student-Led Management	Involves students in democratic decision-making around expectations, discipline, and policies that impact the learning environment. The teacher leverages students to critique and shape all classroom systems.

DOMAIN 3: AUTHENTIC ENGAGEMENT

Authentic Engagement refers to the method teachers use to develop instructional activities and lessons. Effective engagement practices will engage students through five different means: social, intellectual, emotional, physical, and behavioral. The primary goal of authentic engagement is to drive student motivation for learning and provide rigorous learning opportunities that challenge student thinking.

Standard	Title	"The Culturally Responsive Teacher is able to. . ."
3.1	Meaningful Experiences	Plan purposeful experiences that allow students to role play, problem solve, and interact with one another in unique ways. Teacher designs activities that encourage students to create multicultural songs, dances, performances, and presentations.
3.2	Lesson Structure	Apply various instructional strategies (teacher-centered presentations, discussions, demonstrations, activities, etc.) to facilitate students learning. Teacher carefully drafts activities to complement student thinking.
3.3	Differentiation & Rigor	Scaffold the learning from basic to higher order thinking to activate prior knowledge, connect with students of various learning preferences, and support all students to produce high-quality work and solve complex issues.
3.4	Inquiry-Based Learning	Facilitate learning processes that position students as drivers of their own learning and provide multiple ways for students to question and interpret the content they are learning.

Standard	Title	"The Culturally Responsive Teacher is able to. . ."
3.5	Energy & Pace	Utilize their bodies, voices, and facial gestures as teaching instruments to maintain a brisk pace. Teacher models a positive attitude and frequently embeds elements of playfulness and competition into the learning.
3.6	Collaboration	Design learning that creates interdependent relationships amongst students. Teacher structures groups in familiar and unfamiliar ways to ensure that students share important roles and have opportunities to develop expertise.
3.7	Student Discourse	Emphasize teacher-student dialogue through whole group, small group, and peer conversations (discussion, debate, storytelling, reflection, etc.).
3.8	Shared Evaluation	Provide students with the opportunity to evaluate the effectiveness of the lessons as well as determine unique, creative ways to evaluate their academic performance. Learning is assessed by a variety of measures.
3.9	Physical Movement	Implement active engagement strategies to keep students physically and psychologically involved. Teacher uses physical activities to stimulate learning or interest.

Standard	Title	"The Culturally Responsive Teacher is able to. . ."
3.10	Multimedia & Technology	Complement the traditional curriculum with multimedia (examples, newspaper clippings, articles, song lyrics, plays, comics, video games, images, etc.) to spark student interests and curiosity. Teacher provides opportunities for students to utilize technology as a medium to facilitate and demonstrate learning.

DOMAIN 4: SOCIAL JUSTICE CURRICULUM

Social Justice Curriculum refers to the selected curriculum materials and resources in classroom instruction. Effective social justice curriculum will create space for students to discuss histories of oppression and inequality while analyzing current injustices in our society (Darling-Hammond, 2017). The purpose of this domain is to help students reflect on their lived experiences, analyze social issues, and become social change agents.

Standard	Title	"The Culturally Responsive Teacher is able to. . ."
4.1	Self-Concept	Reinforce positive attributes of students' identity and focus on students' values, feelings, and beliefs about themselves. Teacher engages in discussion about how self-concept is influenced by students' sociopolitical context (Individual, Collective, Institutional, and Ideological).

Standard	Title	"The Culturally Responsive Teacher is able to. . ."
4.2	Understanding of Inequity	Equip students with knowledge and understanding of the history of inequality and oppression. Teacher helps students recognize inequity as a result of human-created social and economic relations that can be challenged.
4.3	Cultural Knowledge	Select curriculum materials where students explore a variety of cultures and groups through artifacts, history, etc. Students gain an authentic knowledge and different ethnic groups and an appreciation of diversity.
4.4	Content Relevance	Provide curriculum materials on social, economic, and political issues related to ethnicity, gender, and exceptionality. Teacher plans learning encounters that validate students' lived realities, cultural identities, and heritage.
4.5	Anti-Bias Themes	Structure learning to allow for deep exploration of anti-bias themes. Teacher models how to identify, interpret, and speak out against bias.
4.6	Diverse Perspectives	Use curriculum materials that describe historical, social, and political events from a wide range of racial, ethnic, cultural, and language perspectives. Teacher encourages students to develop multicultural perspectives that respect the dignity and worth of all people.

Standard	Title	"The Culturally Responsive Teacher is able to. . ."
4.7	Social Action	Construct scenarios for students to practice social advocacy skills and utilize tools of activism to become effective change agents in the school and broader community. Teacher assigns activities that challenge students to examine their beliefs and engage in the struggle to make society more equitable.
4.8	Agency	Encourage students to analyze the circumstances of their lived experiences and develop practical tools to persevere through challenges stemming from social injustice.

CHAPTER

1

COMMUNITY PARTNERSHIP

DAVID MCDONALD, M.ED.

> *I am no longer accepting the things I cannot change. I am changing the things I cannot accept.*
>
> —*Angela Davis*

I could not even begin to talk about my experiences as a classroom teacher without first sharing about my experiences as a student myself. I was born in Dallas, Texas, but raised in the neighboring city, Mesquite, Texas, which is a 15-minute drive from downtown Dallas. It didn't take long for me to realize that I would be one of the few Black students in my class. As early as 2nd grade, I started to notice that my classroom experience was different

from the experiences my classmates were having although we sat in the same seats. While most students would advance through their schooling experience with minimal interactions with school discipline, my experience on the other hand, was mostly defined by school discipline. It didn't matter that I was a straight-A student and had almost perfect attendance. It didn't matter that I had been identified as gifted and talented and been considered by my teachers and school leaders for early advancement to the next grade level on multiple occasions. It also didn't matter how involved my mother was in our school's programs or that she always had an active role in our Parent-Teacher Association. But what mattered the most was that I, as a Black boy in a predominately white elementary school, did not think, did not show up, did not speak, and did not learn in the same ways that my white peers did. What started as a few phone calls home for "talking too much," later turned into disciplinary referrals for "disruptive behavior" and "insubordination" from my teachers.

Referrals to the school front office became so routine that there was a desk reserved next to the principal's office for students like me who would end up sitting there for the entire school day. (I guess this was our elementary school's version of in-school suspensions.) This desk was also conveniently located right in the middle of the hallway between the nurse's office, the front reception desks, and the staff bathroom. Consequently, most of my day was spent responding to staff members walking by to use the restroom asking, "what happened this time, David?," as I sat there with all of my work for the day to complete. Every student going to the nurse and every office visitor including parents and even the mailman would see me sitting and would all have the same question. . . *"What did you do?"* It would not be until I became an educator myself that I would find the answer to that question.

There were many factors that contributed to the negative relationship that I had with the system of education early on. Attending a school where neither the administrators, faculty, or staff could identify with the me as a student, the lack of diversity training and identity development given to the teaching profession as a whole, and the absence of culturally relevant curriculum and materials all influenced my interactions with my school and my teachers. It surfaces a memory from the 2nd grade of an end of school year celebration where I can remember the last words I heard from one of my teachers. Imagine a 7-year-old student standing outside the door of a classroom because they have just been kicked out of class. Since it is the last day of school, your teacher is sharing final words to all of your classmates before the summer begins and says "This has been a great year, and I will miss all of you very much. All of you! Except for David out there!" This is a true story and happens to be the most salient memory of my early schooling experiences. Being one of the few Black students who attended my elementary school gave me different challenges. It gave me a new perspective about who the education system was created for and who had been disregarded. Hearing those words from someone you are designated to learn from in school and the person who is supposed to teach you has an impact on your ability to believe that a school is a place for you. That was one of the earliest memories I have of school that impacted my thoughts and beliefs about school for the rest of my life.

I thought that I would never become a teacher or even step foot near the field of education after graduating. But life has a funny way of making us eat our words. It would be 15 years later that I would be standing in my very own classroom as an educator. I look back at those moments from my experience as a student and I use those memories to remind myself of how my action can both positively and negatively impact my students for the rest of their lives. I became an educator because I did not see people who looked like me in the classroom. I did not see teachers who shared the same racial identity that I had; I didn't see myself represented in the curriculum taught and even in the books we read in class. I just felt like school did not represent my background and did not show me reflections of myself through how we learn. I'd always been a child who loved learning and loved finding new things and engaging in projects and experiences. But when it came down to the actual content that we were learning, it just did not excite me. That lack of engagement and excitement in school turned me into a brilliant kid, and when I would finish my work very quickly, I would often get in trouble. My mindset at a young age was when I did not find meaning other than just completing work for a grade in the absence of connection and purpose, I would retreat from the instruction. Can you blame me?

That mindset influenced the ways that I taught as an educator once I entered the field of education and what I would do and would be for my students I knew were sitting in my classroom just like me. Students who might have been bored, or disengaged, or had a teacher who tarnished their relationship with education. My goal was to be the person that I believed I did not have in my classroom. I wanted to be someone who not only could understand that students need to see themselves in their curriculum and in the instruction, but also the person who could give them the space they needed to grapple with who they are in connection to what they were learning about. All of those things are so very important. Those are the experiences that I lacked in my own K-12 experience, which should be brought to the center of the educational experience.

There were so many aspects of my classroom that I believe contributed to the unique culture and memories created. Still, the connection between our classroom and the community is central to the approach I took to my teaching. The examples that I share through the rest of this chapter are by no means an exemplar of a partnership between schools and the community. But instead, it is what I believe is the bare minimum expectation of how we expect educators and schools to work with the community.

COMMUNITY KNOWLEDGE

> **Community Knowledge:** The culturally responsive educator gains critical knowledge about the local community and students' families, including history, culture, and values. Teacher leverages community knowledge to foster a safe and responsive learning environment.

Being raised in the Dallas community gave me so much more leverage in the classroom with how I could set up instruction for my students. It allowed me to bring a new world to my students through enhancing the instruction versus simply teaching the given curriculum. All English Language Arts teachers know that literacy is essentially about reading, listening, speaking, and writing. If that is the core of instruction, it leaves the entire world of literature and life open to exploring. Why would we not use books that connect to the world around our students? By building my community knowledge about the city where my students live in relation to my lived experiences from being a Dallas resident, having my family in Dallas, and knowing a lot about Dallas from my upbringing. It did not stop there. I learned that just because you are from the city, does not mean you know everything about your students' actual experience in that city. I continued to step outside of what I thought I knew to learn more about the Dallas community as a whole and what that looks like and sounds like for my students.

It looks like attending community events, baseball games, and performances put on by the local theatre department. It looks like going to Dallas community meetings or city council town halls to build more of an understanding about what is happening at the city level that may impact our students' lives directly in the classroom and our school environment. It also means using the power of the internet like Google, (yes, Google!) and social media to research the history of the community. I took on an active role to broaden my understanding of the community my students and I came from.

When you build that community knowledge around your students and the city where your students live, you are able to repurpose that into your instruction and content to make an even greater impact on your students. One of the critical things that I could do with my community knowledge was to bring in my network of relationships with people who live in the Dallas community. I knew who the critical leaders in our community were and had been able to build connections from businesses to organizational leaders. Though my students already had some background knowledge of various aspects of the community, they were able to add to building the community knowledge; however, as the educator, I was able to expand their perspective by allowing them to personally meet, see, and hear from these individuals. When I bring those individuals into the classroom, whether as a metaphor, or just an example during my instruction, students are more easily able to access those references because they already have experienced that right in their backyard.

It is also about building those connections so that you continue to learn more about the community in which your students live. You are also able to make some of those more intimate connections with your students. When the time comes to build relationships with students, you have some more context because you've spent time learning about the community to impact them.

FAMILY INVOLVEMENT

Family Involvement: The culturally responsive educator develops trusting relationships with diverse families to maintain involvement throughout the year. Teacher consistently incorporates family input and insight when determining academic goals, curriculum, and expectations.

One of the most critical parts of my approach to teaching was the concept of an open classroom. Creating a space to be flexible and open enough for community members, other teachers, students, and most importantly, families to be able to enter the classroom and become a part of a learning experience at any moment regardless of what was on our "agenda" for the day. Too often, we see in our classrooms where it is almost impossible for parents to visit the classroom and to be able to join in as a part of the learning community outside of meeting the teacher nights and progress report meetings. We close our doors and keep our students inside for those 60 minutes, or however long class is. Creating an isolated island of the learning experience, which leaves our students at a disadvantage. I think that psychologically when we open those doors of our classroom, it generates a breathable place for creativity, imagination, and exploration and we make it possible for the community to access our school.

I remember vividly that at any moment, during my teaching career, parents would pop up with surprises. It may be as small as a birthday party for their child. It may have been a special week for a basketball game and the parents chose to celebrate with the entire class. There may have been a great lesson coming this week because parents have heard about it from their child who is expressing excitement, so they want to come and be a part of the learning. They were welcomed. Students might be making oral presentations in one class period or share some reflections from their journal entries this week. My door was always open. At any moment, anything could happen, and I was ready.

Involving families not only benefits the individual student, but it also benefits the entire class and school environment. Families will feel compelled to show up even when you least expect it. I am thinking about parents like the Johnsons who would always come through for students even if it was the last minute of the day. At the end of the six weeks, the Johnsons wanted to surprise the class with a celebration because they heard how well the students were doing on their work throughout the grading cycle. Yes, of course, they heard from me because I continued to keep the families up-dated, through various forms of communication (more on that later!) They decided to get pizza from the Domino's Pizza down the street from the school. They showed up right near the end of class and blessed the class with a bit of celebra-tion for their perseverance through the hard work that they were displaying in the classroom. That was only possible and only permissible if the classroom was open and the school was available enough to allow parents to join and be a part of the educational environment. Now, it does not have to always be a pizza party, or a huge celebration with balloons and candy, external rewards for the students, you know, that's something that we see a lot, especially in lower grades or just at school in general. Some other ways parents can join the classroom community regularly are by writing encouraging notes to the students, observing instruction for a day or class period, donating necessities for students in need, or simply being a part of classroom or school events through volunteer-ing their time.

As a teacher, I also participated in the home visit project. An initiative established in the Dallas community that allows teachers to get more involved with students' families by visiting their homes and breaking some of those barriers between the school building and home communication. A group of teachers would be asked to select a few students to go to their homes and visit and learn about the student; who they are, what their families and living experiences are like. How they are going about life outside of the classroom. We are not talking about grades. We are not talking about anything behavior-wise. We are not talking about anything other than just learning about the families. What are their interests? What were their hopes and dreams for their child? What are they involved in? What brought them to Dallas? How has their experience been in our schools? Learning more about the families is the entire purpose of the home visit project, and being able to share, of course, just celebrations from the experiences so far with that student. By participating in that project, I was able to learn so much more about my students. It created a completely different experience for that student once we got back into the school building because as an educator, I was able to see them in their natural being outside of the classroom. I was invited into their space and that student-teacher relationship has now been elevated. Therefore, if a student were to act out or struggle emotionally, socially, or academically, I may react differently now that I have a perspective contrary to the view I had of the student only from the classroom experience.

I had one student who I visited during a home visit project that has stuck with me long term. You know, there is always going to be every school and grade level with a particular student that can be a handful at times. A student that other teachers may find challenging to deal with and may not have the tools or the patience to get to the root of the student's problem. Maybe their behavior could be for a plethora of reasons. This student did a complete 180 in terms of their perceptions of our school and even my classroom after I visited their home during the home visit project. I saw the difference almost immediately the next day in the classroom. Initially, this student was not excited about coming to school. They were not enthusiastic about the work they were provided. They would give other teachers pushback about certain things due to a lack of engagement. Based on their experiences of how schools received them as students thus far, they had built up a mindset and attitude around how they were going to show up to the school-house, almost like a defense mechanism because of their negative experience of schooling. Honestly, I cannot blame the student for their response to their learning experience based on my personal experiences in K–12. As I mentioned before, as early as the second grade, knowing how my teachers felt about me as a student and how my turbulent experience was, I was pushed to create my own narrative of how school was going to be for me. In order to protect myself from ever hearing something like that from another teacher again, I chose to defend my experience by controlling my own version of schooling. Therefore, as a teacher, being able to break through those negative experiences for other students and recreate new ones was extremely important.

I digress. Let's go back to my student. That next day coming back into the classroom, it was like a light had just lit inside their head. The student entered the classroom. His enthusiasm showed through his face, through his movements, literally bouncing and dancing as he approached the door. For a brief moment, I almost did not recognize the student. However, he was transformed from being a student who was disengaged in my classroom who refused to do the classwork and collaborate with his peers or was apprehensive about sharing out in the whole group in the classroom. If it were possible, I wish I could embed videos into the book to show you all an example from a drama conducted in class where students practiced reader's theatre. As an educator, the culminating moment for me was seeing him embody a scene from the drama that we were reading. He was open with the character's feelings and held himself to an expectation of perfecting the lines of the character. He modeled the energy of the storyline and drew his peers in to him as the character by making them laugh and applaud as if we were in an actual theatrical experience. He was their number one star. He exhibited a deep understanding of the material by taking it from the written form and depicting the character in a realistic form by using his creativity. I could see that his internal motivation was now activated. It really allowed me to see that growth happening in real time and his experience of school turn into a positive experience. I do attribute that to being able to visit the home of that student. Therefore, my wish is that we can have more educators and our families have these types of interactions and occurrences. It really will shift the culture for some of our students and how they participate with our schools.

What is critical to me is making sure that we contact our parents and allow them to be consistently updated about what is going on in the classroom and in the school environment, how they can be involved, and how their children are doing in our class. Often, I used group messages as one form of communication. This created the village and community necessary to get our students through; to push them to success. In many Black family traditions, we often hear that "it takes a village to raise a child." Therefore, I took that same concept into my classroom to build that community in that village for our students. Something as simple as group messaging using apps such as Google phones or GroupMe allowed for parents to share ideas for lessons, to participate in polling where parents' voices are elevated on critical issues. One instance I was not so sure would work, was when I asked our parents what topics I should include in our classroom discussions. Another example was when I would send some pictures from our lessons so that they could have insight into the classroom experience without having to physically be in the room. Some parents worked long hours and were unable to come up to the school or be as involved as they wished to be; however, they still loved and cared about their child. Therefore, I wanted to find creative ways for the parents to continue to know what was happening in order for the parent to be able to show some love to the student for the student work and activities they were able to view on that day. This also helped generate open communication between the student and the parent when they returned home. From a conversation of when the parent asks the student, how was their day at school to the parent now saying, "Hey! Your teacher sent me a picture of some of the incredible work you guys were working on as a class project, tell me a little about that." I believe that this impacted the family unit, the classroom community, and the relationship between the school environment and the home and allowed the distance between home and school to close.

SUPPORT SYSTEM

> **Support System:** The culturally responsive educator invites family and community members to be active participants in maintaining the social emotional well-being of students. Teacher facilitates opportunities for students to talk about identity, experiences, and other aspects of their lives.

When I think back to my classroom experience as an educator, some of the fondest memories are times that were spent outside of teaching—particularly thinking about the comradery during lunch breaks. I know that lunch breaks are pretty standard for most teachers in having about 30 minutes to eat, take care of your needs, and get ready for your next class. Part of that 30 minutes is spent talking to a colleague about something that needs to be done or going to the office to run an errand and maybe taking a personal phone call or even using the restroom. Perhaps having back-to-back classes and the demands of teaching in general, your time is precious. However, at times I would choose to dedicate some of my precious time to our students and use this time to create a system of support for certain students who are in need. Maybe there is a space where students need to talk about something where the classroom instructional time is not appropriate. Because my school allowed for teachers to create these supportive spaces for our students, I granted access for my students to come into my class during lunch. We would sit and talk about some of the things that were going on in their lives. I would even offer my classroom for mentors during lunchtime to talk with students as their mentees to create those multiple levels of support for the student. Lunchtime became one of the favorite parts of my experiences as a teacher because of the time that I spent with students to simply check in on their emotional well-being outside of structured classroom time. Getting to know them and providing a space where they could relax, let their guard down, and have fun within the same environment that they learnt also allowed me to see these students in a different light. Frequently, I would have almost my entire class still in my room during lunch because they just enjoyed the space so much, both when we were learning and when there was downtime, to be in community with one another. I found that this was therapeutic for me as an educator as well, because I built a supportive collective where students could lean on one another as well as lean on their mentor-mentee relationships in addition to me as the educator.

CONTEXTUAL LEARNING

> **Contextual Learning:** The culturally responsive educator builds bridges of meaning between the classroom and the students' home community. Teacher utilizes real-world events, issues, and information as the basis by which students explore and engage in learning.

One thing that baffled me during my teaching experience was using the field lessons and taking students on field trips to take the lessons and the learnings outside of the classroom. Even in the first school I ever taught at, it was sometimes even hard to get outside of the classroom due to lack of funding or a focus on maximizing instructional time and no outside exploration. There were so many restrictions and focus on structure, from how many kids could be in the hallway and what side of the hall they had to walk, to how much red tape and hoops we had to jump through to receive approval to do extended activities with the students to broaden their perspective outside the classroom. Unfortunately, it limited our ability to create opportunities for contextual learning.

Other than recess and sports activities, how often do we allow students to get outside of the four walls of their classroom to expand their experience? Most importantly, I believe that those field lessons and experiential learning experiences that we can take students on are critical to the students' experience. Creating opportunities where students can engage with the community through volunteering or going to museums, theaters, historical parks, and more are essential to pushing the boundaries of textbook learning.

For example, during my second year of teaching, the then Secretary of Education, Betsy Devos, decided to come and visit our school to see some of the things that we were doing inside the school and the classroom. There happened to be a lot of controversy with educational policy laws and the views of Betsy DeVos. Therefore, when the news started to circulate in the Dallas community that she was coming to visit our middle school, there were a lot of mixed emotions and differing opinions which led to individuals protesting her school visit during this time. There were also those in support of her views who showed up as well. However, despite my personal views as an educator, I was sure that taking this as a learning opportunity for my students would provide them with the tools and skills to respond in an informed manner and be confident in their views of this experience.

I took this as a chance to get our students involved in the things that were going on, why there were people liter-ally on the outside of our schoolhouse with opposing views because of a visit from one person. We have windows, and I knew that the students could see the crowd forming outside of the school. Therefore, I wanted to get them up and moving and in front of the doors of our school. I was going to use this as an opportunity to create some impact with our students. Instead of simply ignoring the crowd of protesters outside and all the news circulating our school about this visit, we turned this real-world experience into a classroom project where students would research some of the controversial policies that the Secretary of Education, Betsy DeVos, favored during her term. Based on their research and our discussions, students were required to create statements that included their personal experience of how the educational policy laws that Ms. DeVos favored impacted the students directly. Approved by the school administration, students would craft their statements, practice with their peers as well as myself, and share those statements during Ms. DeVos's visit to the classroom. Students took on the role of news journalists and reporters to record themselves talking. We created a live press conference in our classroom. We got to have students come up and share their opinions and share what they thought it meant to be a great leader and how someone can be in a position like Betsy DeVos, which significantly impacts our communities. In this context, Ms. DeVos allowed for students to share their voices. I believe that this instilled a sense of pride within the students to not only speak from a knowledgeable perspective about real-time policies that directly impacted them as students, but to speak to those in positions of power who have the ability to change those policies to better serve the community.

The visit from the Secretary of Education, Ms. DeVos, was not the only example that I could use to create contextual learning experiences for my students. Another prominent case that happened within the city of Dallas was that of Botham Jean. Botham Jean was a 26-year-old, Black man who was tragically murdered in his apartment by an off-duty white woman police officer, 31-year-old Amber Guyger, in downtown Dallas who mistook him for an intruder in his own apartment. Officer Guyger reported that after ending a long shift at work, she wrongly entered his apartment thinking it was hers, and shot him point blank range in the chest because she believed he was a burglar. Guyger was convicted of murder for fatally shooting Jean and sentenced to ten years in prison. This happened not too far from our school. Our students heard about this case and had been talking about it; rightfully so. There were feelings of confusion, anger, and resentment, hurt and pain, and so many questions that were circulating the classroom. When tragedies like these happen so close to home, within the community, I find that students struggle with understanding the historical context of these events. Therefore, as the educator, I was thinking about how we could help students process this incident and talk about what was going on in a productive way for them and their learning. I was also thinking about some of the things we could do to help them get involved and be active participants by performing our civic duty in this case.

As Language Arts teachers, there is an expectation that we always incorporate some type of reading and some writing into the lesson to continue to build that skill. Therefore, once we learned about the case and the actual events that led up to the tragic shooting, we first held classroom discussions to allow the students to share their personal feelings about it. This allowed students to bring their lived realities into the space that I believe their peers had never heard. It also allowed me to teach healthy discussion habits when heavy emotions are involved in cases such as these. From there, students reflected in their journals and wrote about the facts of the case as we evaluated the evidence presented by news articles. Once students were able to process their emotions and the events of the case, they were then asked to craft letters to the judge who presided over the case to detail how cases such as these impact the student experience. Students became overly committed to the case and voicing their concerns to the judge. Not only was it relevant to them as a student, but it was also necessary for our community. They also felt like they could lend their voice to create change within their community and beyond. I expressed to them that those letters could be mailed out to State and City Council members to add additional perspective from individuals they may have never heard from before. Those letters could have been included in the impact statements presented to the judge at the sentencing. When we, as educators, open our minds to enhance our instruction and pay closer attention to what is happening in our communities, we add much more value to learning experiences for our students.

As we move forward in community partnerships for our students, the following section is community service. As we continue to ask students to be leaders and step up and be involved in our classrooms, we often do not allow the time to show them how to. We do not give students the same access and ability when it comes to things that directly impact them such as school policies and school board elections where too often, their voices are not sought out. One of the things that I tried to elevate during my time in the classroom was thinking about community service as an outlet to let students explore leadership opportunities, to be involved in the things that directly impact their community.

COMMUNITY SERVICE AND LOCAL PARTNERSHIPS

Community Service: The culturally responsive educator creates opportunities for students to build community through volunteerism that directly benefits the community.

Local Partnerships: The culturally responsive educator is able to partner with local organizations, businesses, and leaders, to maximize learning experiences through guest presentations, interviews, demonstrations, etc.

In addition to enhancing the classroom experience, during 2017, there was a moment for school board elections. I had an opportunity to allow a couple of my students to sit in on some of the candidate forums to give their opinions on the educational policies that the candidates were proposing, in an effort to lend their support based on what they heard from them. This opportunity led to students being able to show encouragement to potential candidates in the form of service, by either writing letters of support, canvassing neighborhoods, and getting people excited to vote during school board elections. In the past, turnout was usually low. However, my students had a direct hand in increasing the voter turnout for the school board elections and shared why they believe in specific policies at the school.

Another experience that will forever stick with me was in my additional role as a Debate Coach at the school. During my first year of teaching, we were able to start the very first debate team at our school. When we created the team, we knew we had novice students who had never debated in any form or capacity before. Therefore, we realized that we had a lot of work to do because historically many of the other debate teams that we would compete against were experienced and able to access resources to build their skills that we were not privy to. Where they may have had an entire class of debate team members, our school was a small, afterschool club run by me and one other teacher who served as a co-debate coach.

We spent hours at the school, practicing and learning about what debate looks like, how you stand and your posture, how to showcase your confidence and elevate your voice, and other techniques of debate. We noticed right away that our students had more flavor, and more swagger in the ways that they talked and the ways that they walked.

They brought their authentic selves to the debate team, and we were sure as coaches not to strip that away from them. However, at their first competition, we noticed that they were not getting brownie points for their authentic selves in the way that we felt like they should have. Debate is very standardized and structured in the way you are expected to look and respond and because we allowed our students not to fit into this box, we felt that they were being penalized for this. Therefore, we wanted to honor our students and truly celebrate all the work they put into their first ever debate competition. So as coaches, we hosted our very own Debate Night for our students. This event entailed our students competing against each other where we invited the entire school, family and friends, and the community. Community members in attendance were invited to participate as judges. We partnered with local organizations such as the Black Chamber of Commerce, the Dallas area Urban League, as well as the Young Professionals organization. We were able to show our students that these are people who look like you, who come from places where you have been, who live in this community, and who work in a community. Let them be your judge and be the ones to decide how well you are doing. It turned out to be a phenomenal event. We had over 300 people attend. Being able to create an experience like that where we truly partnered with the school and other community organizations to put on an event and inform their community in a way that our students would never forget. A service simply from being their authentic selves that they did not know they had.

SUMMARY

Community partnerships are the basis for strengthening the family-school community throughout the academic school year. When the school and the classroom serve as a space that is open and accessible to families, community members, local businesses, and organizations, an exchange of wealth and wisdom occurs. The school becomes a place of hope, not just for our students that we serve each and every day, but for everyone. We should think of the community and the schoolhouse as a collective that drives student success. According to Ready et al. (2002), schools have historically served as a place to "preserve democracy, eliminate poverty, reduce unemployment, ease the assimilation of immigrants to the nation, overcome differences between ethnic groups, advance scientific knowledge and technical progress, prevent traffic accidents, raise health standards, refine oral character, and guide young people into useful occupations." To transform the state of education today, this is a goal that we must strive to return to. Although we are aware that academic success is the priority for all students, there is no way we can get there without community partnerships.

REFLECTION QUESTIONS

Take some time to reflect and make a plan for **Community Partnerships** in your classroom using the guiding questions below:

1. How have you allowed your students to incorporate their community knowledge into your classroom?

2. What local businesses, organizations, and leaders can you reach out to bring to the classroom?

3. How do you believe families and diverse communities add value to your classroom instruction?

4. What opportunities of volunteerism can you think of to build a stronger community inside and outside of the classroom?

CULTURE MANAGEMENT

DANIELLE ROSS, M.ED.

> *Culture, in effect, is about EVERYTHING. It directs behaviors all the time, so it produces outcomes. Culture is a multiplier to MISERY or MAGIC.*
>
> *—Unknown*

Culture, in effect, is about *EVERYTHING*. It directs the way we talk, walk, dress, how we show up professionally, where we choose to live, who we choose to date. It's about everything. It is funny because education is the one place "culture" was never mentioned to me or brought up. However, whether discussed or not, every school, church, club, or classroom has a culture, a vibe, that attracts a particular

crowd or group. My understanding of culture and how it manifests in an environment started within the four walls of my home being raised by a single mother. Writing this book helped me realize how everything we experience in life is connected and explains where we are currently in this moment. My style of teaching can be considered "nurturing," "loving," or "motherly," and that directly relates to the experiences I had with the best teacher growing up, my mother. How I show up for students mimics the way my mother has shown up for my entire life. It's why I set **High Expectations** for them. It's why I teach them the importance of working together, **Collective Responsibility**. It's why I tell them the importance of being themselves, **Authenticity**, and having healthy **Relationships**. It's why I teach them it's essential to care for and organize your space because it helps organize your mind. It's why I create environments for them where they can be themselves and lead naturally, **Student-Led Management**.

Most importantly, it's why I teach them that we must all work together to create the classroom we all enjoy, **Harmony**. The best educators can bring these connections into their work. We realize that every part of our being has something to do with how we show up in the classroom. It is also why those teachers are naturally the most responsive because they understand the importance of knowing the whole child.

Therefore, when I think about culture management and how it lives in the classroom, it first starts with understanding who **you are** and how you bring that into the learning environment. That is when you begin to make connections to different aspects of your students' lives. From the music they listen to, to the places they eat, to worship, you see your classroom as a community where every story and identity is valued. **Culture is embedded in everything we do**. It's easy for us to see how culture exists in our jobs, homes, sports teams, or pretty much anywhere besides the classroom. Culture management is a priority when it comes to creating a responsive classroom. If your culture ain't right, how can you expect students to learn or want to do anything? I know you may be thinking, "Well, my kids like me, so my culture in my classroom is good," and while students liking you is a dividend of successful culture management, there are still aspects that MUST exist for your classroom to be 100% effective. Without culture, you have nothing; no classroom, no academic achievement, no love, just nothing. So, through my experiences, I hope to get you thinking about the type of culture you want to be true about your students in class or school. Because every class, teacher, and student is essential to me, and I want to see everyone win.

> **Culture Management** refers to the teacher's ability to create a positive, inclusive, safe, and productive classroom environment for students. Effective culture management eliminates barriers and creates an optimal learning environment for students to engage with instruction and retain learning. This domain leverages brain-based theories to support the practices to foster, maintain, and rebuild classroom culture.

ESTABLISHING HARMONY

While many teachers use their summer to rest, relax, and travel, and let me be clear, I enjoy a good HOT GIRL SUMMER, but in this work, the grind never stops, so I use my summers to ideate the environment I want to create for my students in the fall. It comes with a lot of reflection and student feedback, which hint, hint, you should get in the habit of doing. Ask your students how they feel in your classroom or school and stop guessing. It is this genuine feedback that helps me be better and to create learning environments that students enjoy. I typically have to start with a **theme** or a **mantra** I want my students to live by that year. In the past, I have used motifs such as #NONSTOP or "Speak Your Truth," and my favorite one, which is the current theme for my school this year, "WE are the VILLAGE." See, I think this way because it is easier for me to do everything else once I am rooted in a goal, a mission, and a focus for the year. Then everything else falls into place. The colors, posters, quotes, assignments, etcetera all come alive once I know the common goal. And with that, I am taking the first step in establishing Harmony in my classroom.

> **Harmony:** The culturally responsive educator nurtures positive emotions in students that will support their learning and ensure that all students feel safe, cared for, and welcomed. The teacher supports students in developing a positive self-image and beliefs about others.

For many educators, Harmony comes as a reward or job well done at the end of the academic school year when the kids adore the teacher and vice versa. You hear, "We are finally a family" or "The kids finally like me." Well, for me, that's too long to wait. I want to establish Harmony in my classroom from day one because with Harmony comes peace, and peace is every educator's dream in a middle school classroom.

So that's why I am big on themes, and I always encourage educators to start there, whether as a school, content area, or grade level, figure out the collective goal or focus that we want to establish with students and start utilizing them on day one. Let me give you an example. Consider the theme, "WE ARE THE GAME CHANGERS."

In my third-year of teaching, I was a grade-level chair. It was such a huge accomplishment because, for the first time,

I was getting the opportunity to establish a culture and build a team. My consideration around the theme we would focus on started with the individuals on my team. I was new to the school, with a fresh perspective, super excited about leading new initiatives and doing something different. By certification, the first-year math teacher on my team had a unique and fresh perspective, having taught in Inglewood and Watts. Watts, Los Angeles, the epicenter of the Watts Riots in 1965, where the goal was to end police brutality, housing discrimination, lower unemployment rates, and inequality in school resources and funding; a place that was built on culture and a people who consistently fought to keep it alive. Then there was the science teacher, a veteran, with one of the most structured and unique classes I had ever seen. She was looking to be on a team that was finally about something; about change. The three of us made up a dynamic team.

Then there were our students, all of whom would be new to the charter school. We would take students from all over the Dallas area since it was not a requirement for the students to live in the surrounding zones in order to attend. We had no information about their backgrounds, academic progress, nor behavior tracks. However, there was something fun about having the opportunity to give these students a fresh start, something new to look forward to. Despite anything that may have happened in their past academic careers, this new year would be a year of hope for them. That is what we were invested in building for these students. Which is where our theme for the academic school year originated, "WE are the Game Changers"! It only made sense! We explained the meaning behind the saying to our families and students on day one because we believed this was the class that would change the game. The game is education and just like any sports reference, if we give our all and stay 100% committed to the goal, we can change the game. While working to ensure there is a pipeline of game changers in education, or community, families, and students were clear that our drive and our focus would be all about them. Going above and beyond average to exceed expectations. That was our dedication to them.

From there, I committed to making the theme come alive in our hallways. From the bulletin boards to the photo wall. I even got my team custom referee shirts. If you asked any of our students what our theme was, they knew, and that is because my team did an excellent job showing them why they were game changers. It reflected in their attitude, you best believe at any school event, the 6th-grade team was the most respectful and polite, but when it was time to do our chants and cheers, that's when you saw us come alive. It was reflected in their work ethic. They never gave up and always strived to do better. It was reflected in their confidence. At any moment we had visitors, our 6th-grade class officers were there to greet them and give them a tour of the campus. Our young students personified the mantra in a way that was recognized by any individual or leader, whether district or regional, that walked through the front doors of our school building.

You see, there was a collective purpose; a mission; a goal, and we all were a part of it. Because we expected the same from each and every individual on our team from the educators to the students, there was no deviation. We all wanted it to be better because of the strength of our start and our understanding of the ultimate goal. That is what Harmony is, an agreement, a collective purpose. Students need Harmony in school. They need to feel a part of the team and have a sense that they are working towards something greater. At times I think we are doing school all wrong. Students travel from core subject to core subject, class to class, feeling isolated and mundane, and there is no connectedness, no Harmony. We must manage the culture of our schools in a way where students gain a sense of pride that exudes Harmony. They see why their success matters for themselves but also for the community at large. When leaders intentionally create Harmony, the students, no matter the age group, will follow and rise to the occasion.

SETTING HIGH EXPECTATIONS AND CLASSROOM SYSTEMS

Let me start by saying this. High expectations are not simply giving students rules and directions to follow. I remember at my new teacher training when I began in the educational field. Everyone was emphasizing having high expectations for students. They defined it as being "stern" or "cold" with students so they would comply with everything the teacher said.

I noticed that there was an absence of the student-teacher kinship, community or two-way street necessary to achieve high expectations. Once I began to practice this one way that I had been given to have high expectations for my students, I felt and looked crazy walking into my classroom unauthentically, trying to be and present myself as someone I was not. As a result, I noticed that it had become difficult to build the type of relationships I wanted to build with my students. Nothing seemed genuine and because I was told we were only seeking compliance when exhibiting high expectations for our students, the inauthentic manner of being matriculated transmitted to the students. When discussing high expectations, we specifically mean your systems, procedures, restorative practices, and incentives. It is not your behavior charts or reflection folders that you have created at the beginning of the year and have not changed or updated based on student data and feedback throughout the academic school year. Setting high expectations embodies a mindset of a teacher who believes that every single one of their students can achieve great things, despite how they may have shown up two or three years prior in another class, despite what another educator may have said about them, despite any negative commentary that they may have internalized from family or society. High expectations are more than simply a checklist of qualities you are seeking from certain students. It starts with the educator first. You set high expectations by first believing that all students can meet them.

> **High Expectations**: The culturally responsive educator explicitly communicates high expectations for students academically and socially. The leader ensures expectations are reflective of students' home culture and identity.

At the start of every class, my students stood on their chairs, and they would recite our classroom mantra that read:

> I am intelligent
>
> I am capable
>
> I can do anything I put my mind to
>
> I matter
>
> You matter
>
> We can, and we will be, world changers.

Students needed to say this every day before we started the class because it set the proper mindset for learning, and it reminded them that regardless of what happened before they entered this classroom, it did not matter. In my class, I saw them as world changers. Why did I want them to believe they were world changers? Because then they knew I believed in them, but it was necessary that they believed in themselves. A world changer doesn't fight, give up, or lose momentum. A world changer believes in themselves, their community, their vision, and their dream.

High expectations are rooted in everything. How students enter the class, how they speak to each other, as well as systems, such as the homework collection process, are intentionally designed to set clear and consistent expectations for students. Unfortunately, educators lose a huge opportunity when they are not intentional and reflective about the expectations they have in their room. Ask yourself why is this important? Why do I want them to do this? One way you can think through this process is by preparing the rationale of why you are embedding high expectations within the makeup of your classroom and explain it to students as you are outlining the systems and expectations in class. In your reflection process, identify unnecessary systems. Do away with those and only keep the systems that have a high impact on the effectiveness of your classroom. And yes, it is okay. Not having a procedure or system for every little thing does not make you a lousy teacher. Not having a rationale and clear purpose for the system does.

Consider leaving some things up for discussion when you are beginning to decide what you want your class or school to look, sound, and feel like. Again, it does not make you a bad teacher if you don't have all of your expectations and agreements lined out on the first day of class. Consider implementing a student voice in this process. Allow them to say the things they want to be true about their classrooms and have them agree to it. It is easier to hold someone accountable to their own words rather than someone else's. Here is an example of the classroom agreements my 6th graders made up in my class:

MRS. SMITH'S CLASSROOM EXPECTATIONS: THE 7 MAJOR KEYS

1. Be ON TIME and PREPARED to Learn.

2. Take ownership of YOUR ACTIONS.

3. RESPECT IS A MAJOR KEY.

4. Use appropriate language: no put downs, cussing, or other inappropriate words neither in our classroom nor in the hallways.

5. Keep hands, feet, and objects to yourself.

6. NEVER GIVE UP, "I Can't" is NEVER an option.

7. Remain POSITIVE, do your BEST, LEARN, and have FUN.

See, they "get" it! All the way down to "Keeping hands, feet, and objects to [themselves]," which before teaching 6th grade I did not think was necessary, but oh boy, it sure is! It was less of me and more of them, which also showed them I believed that they could create high expectations for themselves and hold themselves accountable, and they did. As a teacher, my role is to facilitate and allow students to lead in their natural ways. So, even in this process of creating these expectations, my students led the way. One student served as the scribe, writing down their peer's suggestions, and other students helped facilitate the discussion, while everyone was involved in the process of agreeing to these 7 "Major Keys." Teaching them to sign their contract to expectations solidified their commitment to excellence at the bottom of the paper. It is a beautiful moment for me, as the teacher, to sit back and watch students operate in their strengths, even on the first day of class.

As we continue discussing High Expectations, I must bring up classroom systems here and explain why they are essential. You see, a teacher that does not have a proper plan for the way they want students to engage in their class is allowing the option for students to not be successful. In addition, what story does a teacher tell by not being intentional about how their classroom will operate as a running system? Every big business is intentional about how they want their company to run. There is some type of purpose for how day-to-day operations may affect personnel or customer care, quality of services, and even employment output. Therefore, the same intentionality and thought process that goes into the way you think about your expectations is the same intentionality and thought process that should create systems. Listen, there may be a teacher out there who says, "Systems are not necessary." Know, you are speaking to the choir. Heck, in my first-year of teaching, the only system I had was to "raise your hand when you needed to go to the sharpener." My mindset changed when I realized I was doing my students a disservice when I did not tell them how things operated in this classroom. In a way where we all were very clear of our roles and no one stepped on the other toes, per say. Like a well-oiled machine. I first noticed it when students would randomly get out of their seats to throw away their trash. I would hear myself say, "Why are you getting out of your seat without permission?" However, I also thought to myself, Danielle, did you ever tell them they could not get out of their seats? Was I explicit in my explanation? Did I even consider their response to my correction of the behavior when I was not even clear on what it would be in the first place? So, how could I be upset when they did not operate the way I wanted them to when I never told them. Before you go the route of saying, "Telling students what to do and how to do it is oppressive," I would like for you to try going to a classroom where no systems exist and explain to me how the way students operate in that class isn't oppressive. Don't worry. I'll wait. I am sure there are plenty of videos on YouTube.

All jokes aside, make the systems, teach students the systems, and explain why these systems are essential and how they help the classroom run like a fully functional, operating machine. I hope you are still with me and connecting to how all of these things matter to building a positive culture management system for students. It is the little things that count in how we want our schools to feel. There is so much positivity that comes from a classroom or school where students know what is expected of them, and they operate in a way that shows high self-respect for themselves and the

school community at large. Here are some examples of procedures you may want to create to guide students in their
classroom:

Arrival/ Entering classroom	1. Greet teacher at the door 2. Grab your materials and sharpen pencils if needed 3. Turn-in any homework assignments 4. Place backpack in designated location 5. Set-up your desk to be ready for the lesson 6. Follow instructions for beginning activity
Homework	Place homework into the homework bin immediately when entering the room. Homework will be returned with grades to students. Students should keep all work until final grades are received. Students will also be given updates on grades and should check accuracy of scores in the gradebook prior to final grading submission.
Borrowing materials from students	If borrowing pencils or materials from another student, no one else should hear you ask to borrow that material.
Where to find assignments (if late/absent)	Locate the "Absent Work" files and pick up assignments from the day(s) you missed. Please talk with the teacher for further details about assignments and for help with work. For homework that was assigned on the day that you missed, you will get two school days for every day missed to complete the assignment.

When a student has a question	I greatly encourage asking questions. We also are about creating a generation of problem solvers. Here are the steps when you have a question:
	Think to yourself about possible answers/solutions
	Check the board and your resources (Student Notebook, Word walls, Anchor Charts, Dictionary, etc.)
	Ask a neighbor or a friend
	[If necessary] Research information
	Then. . . Quietly Raise Your Hand for Teacher Assistance

ORGANIZING YOUR SPACE

During my mother's lectures about keeping the house and my room clean, she would always say, "Your space says a lot about who you are as a person. What do you want people to think about you?" At the time, I did not realize how this would carry me to understand that the space I created reflected the person I was, and this was very true when it came to my classroom. I have seen many classrooms over the years, and one thing I always noticed was that the classroom always took after the teacher. For example, Mr. Hill, a 6th-grade history teacher, who could be described as "nerdy" and well, "boring," has a classroom where students sit in rows facing the front. He did have pictures of Black and Brown leaders on the wall and one bookshelf in the back full of all his favorite African American authors. The goal in his class was for students to pay attention and, most of the time, be quiet, so they could learn from him. As soon as I walked into his classroom, that is the energy I felt first-hand.

Then there was Mr. McDonald, the 8th-grade reading teacher. Mr. McDonald could be described as "energetic," "fun," and "creative." In his classroom, students sat in groups, with each table named after a powerful symbol. His theme was "Leaders of Today, Legends of Tomorrow," and his classroom mantra tied in tightly with this theme. You could see images of Black and Brown leaders in his classroom, including the very students who sat in his class. There was also a subtle combination of red, green, and black, like the Pan-African flag. The goal in Mr. McDonald's class was for students to collaborate and see representations of themselves. As soon as I walked into his classroom, that is the energy I felt.

Now, let me ask you. As a student, which classroom would you rather be in? Which teacher do you already like more? In which classroom do you think you will learn the most? I do not ask these questions to be funny or sarcastic because, for some, there may not be anything wrong with Mr. Hill's classroom, and you are right. There isn't. However, when we think about the experience we want students to have as a result of the space we create, which classroom produces a more positive classroom culture? There is no coincidence that Mr. McDonald's students were the highest performing in the district while Mr. Hill maintained his 56% passing rate, which was simply good enough for him. It is not a coincidence that Mr. McDonald had the highest student satisfaction scores at the end of the year compared to Mr. Hill, who scored about 9th on the campus. Have I proven my point? Your classroom is a reflection of YOU. What do you want students to feel when they enter your space?

> **Organization of Space**: The culturally responsive educator establishes a physically inviting classroom where decor, posters, flags, and other educational materials featured throughout the classroom reflect the cultural diversity of the students and the school community. The teacher arranges classroom space optimally for social interactions including small group discussions, presentations, movement, and teacher-student collaborative space.

DESK SETUP

Arranging student desks and other furniture is a critical component of organizing your space as well. The way you set up your desks is vital to how your class will run. For me, my students always had to be in groups because this meant fewer papers to pass out and more of an opportunity for student collaboration. Some teachers tend to avoid this setup because it creates too much opportunity for students to talk without permission but, why avoid the inevitable? Leverage the opportunity for students to collaborate about your content and topics in class. I have even given students opportunities at the beginning of class to have a "social minute" because they deserve a chance to catch up with their peers just like we do as adults.

Having students in groups also presents the opportunity for **Student-Led Management**.

> **Student-Led Management:** The culturally responsive educator involves students in democratic decision-making around expectations, discipline, and policies that impact the learning environment. The teacher leverages students to critique and shape all classroom systems.

I will discuss this more later, but specifically, as it ties into the organization of space, it creates an opportunity for student-led roles, where students are the center of the decision-making process in your classroom. These roles are not just your "materials manager" or "timekeeper"; it goes beyond that. For example, the *Accountability Leader* makes sure everyone in their group has what they need to be successful on the assignment for that day. They also make sure students are on task and finishing their work. Then there is the *Organization Leader*. This student's job is to make sure the space and materials are kept for their group. This also means that they were responsible for ensuring the space was left better than they found it, organized, and all materials were ready for the next class. Every student played a role, and all students were accountable for a group, a team, a name, or symbol. There is power in this type of system. It shifts the ownership of the learning space from just the responsibility of the teacher, who most often is the center for all learning, to the students, who do not often get the opportunity to have these responsibilities. It instills pride in all students, but specifically those students who may struggle with reading, or have challenges speaking aloud to the group, who are seeking their place of belonging in the learning environment.

After you decide on having students in various types of groups for consistent collaboration, then you will see that your culture management is 100% better. Take the extra step and think about group names to inspire a collective effort. In my first year of teaching, my group names were Black and Brown celebrities, people that I believed that my students could connect with such as Tupac, Selena, Oprah Winfrey, and Drake, for example. I'll admit reflecting on it. The goal was to produce collective effort and work responsibility. Each one of these icons, whether past or present, represented a cultural shift in media and music and I knew my students would recognize the symbolism in their groups which made them even more excited to engage in the learning. As time went on, I shifted to using powerful characteristics as my group names, such as Excellence, Power, Courage, and Loyalty. Students eventually embodied their group names in a way that built character inside and outside of the classroom. Imagine a student, when asked, "What group do you belong to in Ms. Smith's class?" And they respond, my group name is "Courage! I am courageous in everything that I do and even when I get fearful at times, I believe that I can because I have teammates who are just as bold and brave as I am!" Thinking about all of this brings me joy as I reflect on the experiences students had due to the intentionality of the space created by me, their teacher. It all matters! You are not just limited to having students sit in groups to facilitate meaningful student collaboration. Consider a U-shape desk arrangement to promote discussion or even table pairs for a lesson where students will need the help of a partner. A lot of student frustration or disengagement comes from students feeling like they have to do the assignment or project on their own and when they struggle, they do not have the tools and skill to endure. Partnership and collaboration in the classroom fosters strength and once students realize they are not in this alone, you will definitely see a positive impact on engagement.

Additionally, it is okay to change your space multiple times a week. I loved the look on my student's faces as they walked into

> As you read this, stop at this moment. Take out a piece of paper and draw different ways you want to set up your classroom. Then, think about what type of lesson would match the setup: heavy discussion, groups for the win. Socratic seminar, U-shaper is a way to go. Direct instruction for new material, rows that are connected and facing the front is a win! Regardless of how you think about it, the way you arrange your desks matters.

the classroom and noticed that there was a new desk setup. I would hear them say, "What are we going to do today?" or "Yay, we are doing something fun" even if it was just going to be going over test responses, there was joy in the way they sat, something new and different to look forward to, something that caught them off guard.

MATERIALS MANAGEMENT

The last piece of organizing your space is thinking about where your materials live and how students access them daily. This is another reason why I prefer my classroom to be in groups. It is easy to organize materials because everything lives in the group. When I place my materials out for students, I practice collecting and returning the materials just as a student would to ensure that the process is seamless. If I notice something that is not seamless, I change it to make the process easier for the students and me. Where there is confusion, there tends to be chaos and managing your materials is one of the areas we want to ensure has as little chaos as possible. Therefore, this is a practice you should try as a teacher. After you place all of your materials out and you have gone through how students will get what they need daily, try acting it out as a student. This is meaningful when thinking about maximizing class time and making sure students can gather what they need in ample time. Think about all parts of your classroom, from storage of materials to where students go to sharpen their pencils. All of this matters to the classroom as a system. As you think about student materials and organization systems, make a list of systems that need to exist in your classroom. Here is a list of systems and procedures you may want to create for your students.

- **Entrance procedure:** Think about what materials students need access to daily and how they will get them upon entering your classroom.

- **Pencil sharpening procedure:** Even if you think you do not need this procedure, let me be the first to let you know that you do.

- **Paper pass in and out procedure:** Something as simple as the way we pass out papers can leave room for confusion, disruption, and wasted class time. Think about this as a system that can happen without you.

STUDENT-LED MANAGEMENT

As I wrap up this piece around classroom organization and setup, I want to talk about student-led management systems. Let's imagine two classes, Classroom A and Classroom B. Classroom A is heavily centered around the teacher. The teacher passes out the materials, picks them up, and organizes them. The teacher is primarily responsible for the redirection of student behavior and pretty much makes all the decisions in the classroom. When there is an opportunity for feedback, the teacher is happy to give students feedback on their work or anything else about the class; however, the teacher never allows or opens the opportunity for students to provide feedback to either the teacher or their peers. Respect in this classroom looks like the students are compliant with the rules without an understanding of the why behind them, and little to no discussion about the impact of instruction on their learning. Students often do not talk about the content or experiences in the classroom beyond the time they are together within the classroom.

Classroom B is very loud, but productive. Students are constantly having conversations in class, about the task, of course. Students have roles in the classroom. You can see one student organizing the materials at each table, another student welcoming their classmates as they enter the room, and even a student redirecting off-task behavior. Reminding their peers, "You have 5 minutes to finish the Do Now." In this classroom, the teacher often asks students how they want to engage in their lessons. The teacher facilitates a short conversation, and the students choose. There are also many opportunities for students to give feedback. The teacher asks every day at the end of class, "How would you rate today's learning experience?" Students share their feedback, and the teacher adjusts accordingly. Students often have discussions around their experiences in class beyond class time. Some students even connect in the evening to go over missed notes to help their friends stay on top of things.

Again, I use these two examples to describe the experience students are having in these classrooms. Neither classroom is considered "bad" or "wrong," but there is a stark difference between the two. Student ownership: a GIFT that every teacher should cherish. It is the "this is how we do it" attitude that every student embodies, even in your absence. Student-Led Management makes this mentality exist. Allowing students to lead in their natural strengths while also leveraging the different skills students bring into the environment. When students feel a part of the success of a classroom, they are more likely to take ownership of what is accomplished in that environment. Your classroom should be a space where students feel a part of the environment. You do this by giving them roles and bringing them in on important decisions that need to be made. Student-Led Management teaches students responsibility, commitment, and courage. When you have a role, you understand that what you do matters to making this space thriving. As you begin to brainstorm different ways students can lead in your classroom, here are some roles we have found helpful in the past.

- **Paper Leader:** Responsible for passing out all important information students need for class. Also responsible for making sure everything is prepared and ready for the next class.

- **Academic Leader:** Reads the learning focus for the day and facilitates checks for understanding with the class to assure they know what is to come. During class, this leader also supports other students in understanding the concepts of the lesson.

- **Team Captain:** A nominated role by the class. This student meets every student at the door and welcomes them in. The student is also responsible for assuring everyone is on tasks and works hard during the lesson.

You can do as many roles as you feel are necessary for your classroom environment. That is the fun part! You can also choose to nominate or select student leaders. When I utilize this in the classroom, I do both. I select students based on their leadership in class, and sometimes I allow them to run in classroom leadership campaigns while their peers vote for the best candidate. However, do you know what the best part about student-led roles in the classroom is? It is the fact that YOU HAVE LESS TO DO! When you can count on your students to run the show without you, what a relief that is.

THE WRAP UP

So, I know you may be thinking, "The Wrap-Up! We are just getting started!" And I agree with you. There is so much more we can talk about on this topic of Culture Management. Maybe I will save the rest for another book. Perhaps, we will see. If you do not read anything else in this book, at least read this section because you can rest assured that without these critical things, you can kiss the thought of becoming a responsive teacher goodbye! These critical components of Culture Management are **Collective Responsibility, Relationships, and Authenticity**.

> **Collective Responsibility**: The culturally responsive educator creates a community-centered learning environment where students are expected to be individually and collectively accountable for successes and failures. The teacher structures environments for cooperative learning and group activities.

> **Relationships**: The culturally responsive educator processes of establishing meaningful interpersonal relationships with all students and fostering healthy interactions between students. Teacher-student relationships extend beyond the bounds of the classroom as the teacher shows genuine interest in each student.

> **Authenticity**: The culturally responsive educator celebrates the social, cultural, and linguistic differences among students openly and explores these differences with students. The teacher encourages students to represent themselves authentically (verbal communication, body language, cultural expressions, etc.) and they model this with students.

These three live together because you cannot have one without the other to create the optimal environment for students. Here is how I see it. If you choose (and I say choice because all of this is a choice) to bring your whole self into the classroom, speak your truth, and allow students to bring theirs, you are **authentic**. This authenticity leads to strong **relationships** with students as you get to know one another and build a bond, teacher to student and student to student. When you have connections, you have everything. And with everything, you foster **collective responsibility**. Where everyone has each other's back, and no one turns on the other! You literally cannot have one factor without the other because they work together to produce magic.

A FINAL STORY

If you cannot be yourself in your classroom, what's the point? Remember, at the beginning of this section. I talked about my first learning experiences coming from my mother. I brought this to the forefront because it is who I am and how I came to be that way. As educators, the best thing we can do for students is to "be ourselves." Don't worry, it seems complicated to do, but if we can commit to it, the results are remarkable. For example, in my class, we have many discussions about anything and everything: Immigration, pop culture, government elections, you name it! One day, during the reading of *Esperanza's Rising*, there was a discussion about the "border" and what its depiction in the text represented:

freedom. Some students had different understandings of this and, as their authentic selves, wanted to know more. One student, a Black male, raised his hand and said, "Well, if they cross over the border without documentation, doesn't that make them illegal?" My chest sank to my stomach, and I felt an urge to respond, but I did not, and what happened next was unbelievable. Another student, a LatinX female, reacted quickly. "Well, if they made the process easier, no one would have to sneak over! My family struggled to get here, only to arrive with nothing and nowhere to start. We have worked for everything we have, and so NO, crossing the border doesn't make us ILLEGAL!" Other students comforted her, but I appreciated the apology from my male student, who did not fully understand the breadth of the topic. I wanted to cry at that moment because as I watched the students facilitate the conversation amongst themselves, I realized how I had fostered an environment where students could be their authentic selves. Enough to understand each other and walk away with a better understanding of each other's cultural background and journey.

You see, authenticity means you do not have to sugarcoat things with your students because they respect and understand each other. Everything is not perfect, but there is a level of respect that allows them to be their genuine selves. Through me as their teacher, you see, allowing them to be themselves, they spoke up for what they believed, even if it meant others would not understand them. Within that, there is a **collective responsibility** to see each other through true windows and mirrors. Where I, as the educator, am allowing a student to not only learn about themselves through discussion, exploration, and text, but also through mirrors, for the students to discover more about others who are different from themselves. That is what the ultimate classroom culture looks like to me. They learn just as much from me as I learn from them while also learning from one other.

SUMMARY

Culture Management, not to be confused with classroom management, is the process by which the educator cultivates an environment of shared success, shared challenges, and shared triumph, where students understand that the learning environment is not only about academic achievement but is also about character development and community building, where the priority of the classroom is everyone's responsibility to ensure that the classroom is operating at its maximum functionality. Where the teacher is no longer the center of the classroom. Culture management does not mean that we negate the academic expectation of our students. It means that to ensure that our students, specifically students of color, will attain academic victory, we must ensure that we are permitting them to bring their authentic selves into the classroom while we, as educators, model that authenticity for them where our students are eager to lead their peers and know that they are just as accountable for the management of the classroom as their teachers are. The students understand that collectively we are stronger as a unit than we are as individuals, so think about it like this (Parker, 2003). Every district and campus's vision statement is designed and created by leadership teams and administration staff. Once this vision is crafted and shared with the school community, the idea is that every educator, every staff member, and every individual that serves students becomes invested in a shared vision. The district may attempt to build this investment through professional development, team builders, and staff retreats to ensure that every individual employed in the district is on the same page. Now, let's take this same concept and apply it to our classrooms. Crafting a shared vision and ensuring that each individual who walks into that classroom environment is invested into the community, into the culture, into the way that you all work and operate every day, which is key to a sound, culturally responsive class-room (Revell, 2021).

REFLECTION QUESTIONS

Take some time to reflect and make a plan for **Culture Management** in your classroom using the guiding questions below:

1. In what ways have you often mistaken culture management for classroom management?

2. How have meaningful, interpersonal student-teacher relationships challenged or affirmed your position as an educator?

3. In what ways have you authentically celebrated culture in your classroom?

4. How do your classroom systems and routines reflect diversity, equity, and justice?

AUTHENTIC ENGAGEMENT

ANDRE ROSS, M.ED.

We must remember that our students are innately creative, innovative, and collaborative and that we suppress these things with our control. Empowerment is the key that will unlock them.

—Kevin Parr

---

engaged (v.)

- **To occupy, attract, or involve (someone's interest or attention).**

- **To cause someone to become involved in.**

NO PLACE IS AS ENGAGING AS THE BLACK CHURCH

As a young, Black kid growing up in a Christian home, I learned everything I needed to know about authentic engagement from the Black Church. Some kids tell their parents, "I don't want to go to church—it's BORING!" at an early age, but my siblings and I were different. Number one, we were saved—for real, but also, we never had a dull moment attending church. From the harmonious choir performances to the high **energy and pace** of a praise break with unison clapping rhythms, jingling tambourines, washboards being scraped with a fork, and members of the congregation catching the Holy Spirit in a way that makes them take off running, **physical movement**—church service just always felt like the place to be. My siblings, Tone, Alyssa, and I were so engaged and so involved in the service, that we would reenact the entire service when we got home as a way to hold on to the experience and the joy we felt. My brother would be beating the drums and repeating lines he heard the pastor say in service, I would pretend to be my great-aunt and play the piano (aka pat my fingers on the family room table with an occasional dance of praise in between), my sister would have the baby tambourine and we would sing and shout as if we had a congregation ourselves. It is funny thinking back on those memories. Still, I remember them so vividly today because that is what it looks like to have been fully engaged—to have had such a **meaningful experience** that you can recreate the memory on your own.

As we grew older, it became less about imitation and more about becoming involved in the church and our services. Each service had its **structure** that helped us see how we could play a particular role. My brother, Tone, was good at playing the drums—so that is how he served, Alyssa has a beautiful voice and held it down in the choir, and I was getting to the bag, as usual, working on the finance committee. Essentially, all three of my siblings and I had a ministry in our church to **collaborate** and have **discourse** with other church members and give perspective, **shared evaluation,** on how our ministries can improve. My parents ensured that there was not a Sunday that went by that my siblings and I would not be in Sunday School by 9:30 am, nor bypass a summer where we were not in Vacation Bible School. Those experiences are where I first learned how **differentiation, rigor, and inquiry-based learning** taught the same messages and themes from the larger service, but in a way that my teenage friends and I could understand and explore further. Even in this day and age, some of the most well-known and popular Christian preachers and ministers are known for differentiating their congregations using **multimedia, technology,** and other props to cement full audience engagement and understanding.

We have many moments in our lives, but not all of them are memorable. The difference between a moment and a memory is how engaged we were in that moment—was it impactful and meaningful enough for our brains to store it? Think about the most engaging experiences you have had in your academic career—what are the patterns, similarities, and themes? Gleaning lessons from the Black Church is a start but let's take it back to the classroom for an example.

> **Authentic Engagement**: The culturally responsive educator develops instructional activities and lessons. Effective engagement practices will engage students through 5 different means: social, intellectual, emotional, physical, and behavioral. The primary goal of authentic engagement is to drive student motivation for learning and provide rigorous learning opportunities that challenge student thinking.

COLLABORATION, STUDENT DISCOURSE, AND SHARED EVALUATION

One of my most memorable teaching experiences came in my very first year. I was so excited about the lesson I planned to teach—my most engaging yet! I was a 7th-grade mathematics teacher, and I assigned the students a group assignment where they were tasked with collaboratively creating a word problem and an answer key for the problem. The other students in the class would solve the problem.

Each student had a role in their group to execute, which was essential to completing the project. It was one of my most memorable lessons because, to this point, I had never seen students have so much meaningful conversation about the content. Their ability to make connections to their own experiences was on full display. There are five different types of student engagement, and this lesson was designed to engage students in all five:

- **Intellectually** - displaying their skill with the content and verbally sharing their findings

- **Emotionally** - connect their feelings and morals to the assignment

- **Socially** - interactions with peers and collaboration during the assignment

- **Culturally** - personal experiences and identity driving their creativity

- **Physically** - physical movement collecting supplies and gathering with their group

The greatest myth in classrooms worldwide is that teachers hold all of the knowledge and students are like buckets for us to pour our knowledge into. Unfortunately, this myth has produced lecture-style, "sit-and-get" type lesson structures devoid of essential engagement elements. Trust me; I am not pointing fingers because I was guilty of employing the same teaching style early on in my career. However, at a certain point, I realized that we were not going to achieve our collective class goals with that mindset towards teaching and learning. At that moment, I decided to take just a few more hours of my time to intentionally and thoroughly plan for collaborative learning and make student discourse a norm and a characteristic element of my lessons.

> **Collaboration:** The culturally responsive educator designs learning that creates interdependent relationships amongst students. The teacher structures groups in familiar and unfamiliar ways to ensure that students share important roles and have opportunities to develop expertise.

> **Student Discourse:** The culturally responsive educator emphasizes teacher-student and student-student dialogue through whole group, small group, and peer conversations (discussion, debate, storytelling, reflection, etc.)

The most important thing to consider when planning for collaboration and discourse is giving *clear, concise, student-centered directions* on collaborating and engaging in discourse. This may be the part where you try to tune me out with a "yeah, yeah, yeah, Andre. I know that already," but please hear me—this is not as obvious as you might think. This was a hard reality for me to deal with early on because my natural personality is laid back and relaxed. However, the first time I assigned a project like the one I described earlier, I quickly learned that laid-back and relaxed instructions were going to produce a lot more work for me on the backend. I would be walking around answering the same questions 20 times because my directions were confusing, which caused a delay to the start of the assignment, more talking out of turn, and difficulty maintaining our noise level. Save yourself time and frustration by giving instructions that are clear, concise, specific, and student-centered and by checking students' understanding of the directions before releasing them to complete the assignment.

Successful collaborative activities also require that each person in the group have a role in the project's success. Allow me to use another extended analogy to help illustrate this point. Some of the best collaborators that we can look to of all time are team-sport athletes. During Spring 2020, Michael Jordan released a documentary called *The Last Dance*. It followed the Chicago Bulls' journey through their domination of the NBA in the 1990s and specifically their "last dance" season in 1998. There were several themes and takeaways from the 10-part docuseries, but what I walked away with thinking is that even on the greatest teams, you still need EVERYONE to star in their role—whatever that role may be. Michael Jordan got a lot of praise because his role was to score as much as possible. However, the Bulls could not have won their championships without a man named Dennis Rodman, whose job was not really to score—or even shoot. His role was to get as many rebounds as he could and play strong, tough defense. Mike and Rodman were both essential to the team but had completely different roles to play. Thankfully they had one of the most innovative coaches to help manage their personalities and clarify the importance of each role. You probably think, what in the world does this have to do with my classroom—I am glad you are still reading. Here it is:

I used to think of myself as if I was Phil Jackson, that great Bulls dynasty coach. I set the lineup (assign the groups appropriately) and ensure that each person understands fully and can be a star in their role. Rewind to my classroom example where the students were creating their rate of change word problems. The first thing that I had to do was decide how many roles there would be for the project. The roles I decided on were:

- 2 Scribes who collaborate to create the problem and poster

- 2 Solvers who create the solution(s) poster with the answer key for students to check their work

- 1 Presenter who shares on behalf of the group for the oral presentation

It is simply a coincidence that there were five students in each group, just like a basketball team. Each role was made intentionally to ensure that each person had a vital role in the success or failure of the project. There were no empty roles like coloring the poster or someone to get the materials. Each person had a role that was tied to a portion of the rubric. Once I decided on how many students were going to be in each group, I differentiated my groups by mixed skill levels, 1 High, 2 Medium, 2 Low. Another major key when it comes to setting groups up for success is personality compatibility. It may be worth combing through your groups a second time to ensure that all vibes will be positive during the assignment behaviorally. Lastly, but most importantly, as the Phil Jackson of my classroom, I made sure that each student understood their role. To do so, I printed role sheets with descriptions as well as step-by-step directions for each role while I verbally explained the expectations for each role before releasing them to work.

Steps to Prep for Collaboration & Discourse

1 Decide how many student roles you need for each group

2 Differentiate and preassign the groups based on mixed skill level and compatibility

3 Create role sheets with a description of the responsibilities of each role

4 Verbally explain each role before releasing students to work

---

The extra steps that I took to prepare for collaboration and discourse are accountability measures so that students would make the most of the project. Speaking of accountability, my favorite portion of the assignment was giving students the responsibility of evaluating each person in their group based on the project rubric and role sheet. The most powerful form of accountability is from student to student, especially when they are sharing responsibilities on a project. Also, there is no deeper level of engagement than facilitating a project where students must be engaged in their portion of the project and everyone else's. The increase in student ownership benefited my class for that one assignment and throughout the rest of that school year. As we know, student ownership begets student engagement, and student engagement produces academic performance. We all love a win-win situation.

> **Shared Evaluation**: The culturally responsive educator provides students with the opportunity to evaluate the effectiveness of the lessons as well as determine unique, creative ways to evaluate their academic performance. Learning is assessed by a variety of measures.

When it comes to shared evaluation, most educators are comfortable allowing students to evaluate their own academic performance. Still, they are uncomfortable with students evaluating their performance as a teacher or sharing their opinion on an individual project. As an educator, it could only make you uncomfortable for a few reasons: either (1) the educator does not care about the students' opinion, (2) the educator is afraid of the students' opinion of them/their assignments, or (3) the educator has no plans on improving their instructional capacity and skill set. Students are the most valuable resource and most unbiased evaluators for educators. Once I was able to get my ego in check, it opened doors to relationships with students that I had never had before. It also made me a better man and teacher because I did not allow my pride nor status to hinder me from asking for feedback. If students' opportunities to give feedback in your class are few and far between, I encourage you to design multiple feedback systems to share their thoughts and perspectives freely (Banks and McGee, 2020). You will accelerate your development and growth in this field by doing so. There are many ways that teachers can accomplish this goal whether you are looking for quick feedback or set up an extensive system for gathering your students' opinions on their experience. Here are a few:

1. Use a Google Form or paper survey to collect anonymous data from students once or twice per quarter

2. Empower a group of students to collect evidence from the class each semester and provide the class with a summary of their findings along with potential solutions

3. Check in with each individual student at least once per semester to ask open-ended questions that unearth their feelings about their progress and experience in class

LESSON STRUCTURE AND INQUIRY-BASED LEARNING

Lesson structure is the aspect of a lesson plan that has a clear guide and direction of how the instruction will be delivered. Many teacher education prep programs, as well as Districts, teach that your lesson *must* include:

- "I-Do" - teacher models a concept for the class.

- "We-Do" - teacher models a concept for the class based on the direction of one or more students

- "You-Do" - students model that they have understood the concept by completing a practice question on their own

- Independent Practice - students complete a full set of similar questions to show their understanding and mastery of the concept.

Now let me just stop and give a disclaimer. If you are new to the profession, and your coach just taught you this structure, I am not saying not to use it. This framework is a great place to get started, but plenty of other lesson structures and frameworks yield more engagement, enrichment, interest, and higher performance.

The lesson structure mentioned above can be limiting for many reasons, but at the top of that list is the exclusion of a hook and an "explore" activity. I could not have written a chapter on Authentic Engagement without mentioning two of the most critical aspects of the lesson structure that often go overlooked. The hook is used to spark student interest in the topic of the day in class and the explore activity is used to activate their prior knowledge connected to that topic. By excluding the hook and the explore sections, we assume that students have no foundation to build from—that they are an empty canvas and vessel. However, that's the biggest mistake any educator can make. We often find that students' greatest struggle on standardized assessments is the ability to use their schema or background knowledge to answer the questions. Well, if we avoid building their knowledge within the set instructional time, how can we expect them to use it?

> **Lesson Structure**: The culturally responsive educator applies various instructional strategies (teacher-centered presentations, discussions, demonstrations, activities, etc.) to facilitate student learning. Teacher carefully drafts activities to complement student thinking.

I like to think about our students like computers. When a consumer goes into the Apple Store to purchase a brand-new MacBook computer, it comes with certain items already programmed in which are the most commonly used software. It is capable of connecting to the internet, printing documents, email, and so forth. As computer owners, our role is to make sure that this computer is connected to the power source and additions to the software needed to complete our projects. It is the same for our students—they have prior experiences, lessons learned from their upbringing, and prior knowledge from previous academic years that are probably valuable to them individually and to their classmates when trying to learn a new topic. If we ignore the software already programmed in our students, it is just like forcing your new computer to download new software when there is compatible software already installed.

The "I-Do, We-Do, You-Do" structure is also limiting because it is incapable of accounting for the multiple ways that problems could present themselves, nor for the multiple strategies that could be used to find the solution(s). So the question becomes how do we account for this level of variability within topics? Yes, you guessed it—this is where Inquiry-Based Learning comes into play.

> **Inquiry-Based Learning:** The culturally responsive educator facilitates learning processes that position students as drivers of their own learning and provide multiple ways for students to question and interpret the content they are learning.

Utilizing inquiry in your lesson promotes authentic engagement, and it also encourages student curiosity and experimentation. When I began my teaching career, one of the phrases I would often hear was, "we need to shift the cognitive load from teacher to student." I was one of those teachers who knew my content well, so my lesson became more about showing students what I know instead of facilitating discussions, experiments, and activities to show me what they were learning and grasping the concepts for themselves. On a very surface and fundamental level, I understood the importance of "shifting the cognitive load," but I was still unsure of how to do so. Luckily, I had a coach who cared about my development as a teacher who helped me begin to unpack how I could implement as much inquiry-based instruction (Pedaste et al., 2015) into my lesson plans as possible.

ESSENTIAL COMPONENTS OF INQUIRY BASED LEARNING	DESCRIPTION
Orientation/Observation	The teacher introduces a new topic or concept. Students explore the topic through research, direct instruction, and hands-on activities.
Question/ Conceptualization	Students develop questions related to the topic, make predictions, and hypothesize.
Investigation	This is the lengthiest part of inquiry learning. Students take the initiative, with appropriate teacher support, to discover answers, to find evidence to support or disprove hypotheses, and to conduct research.
Conclusion	Having collected information and data, students develop conclusions and answers to their questions. They determine if their ideas or hypotheses prove correct or have flaws. This may lead to more questions.

Discussion/Sharing	All students can learn from each other at this point by presenting results. The teacher should guide discussions, encouraging debate, more questions, and reflection

OBSERVATION & CONCEPTUALIZATION

It all started with the topics. For inquiry-based learning to help engage students, we as teachers should build a strong understanding of what may be relevant or enticing to the specific groups of students that we serve. As such, I suggest that you sift through all of the standards that you teach to find connections to current or historical events that students may explore more deeply. If there are not any current or historical events that apply, we must use the most powerful gift that we all have access to, our imaginations. Accessing our imagination as adults and modeling that behavior could be the key for students to learn this process of understanding new and unfamiliar content.

Inquiry-based learning places the responsibility for learning back onto the students. Teachers play a significant role in guiding the discussions that students will have, monitoring student dialogue to address any misconceptions that arise, and adding information to accelerate students' further thinking on the topic. One of my favorite inquiry lessons to teach was an 8th Grade mathematics lesson that covered graphical transformations: translation, rotation, reflection, and dilation. This lesson was on a Friday after spending the rest of the week skill-building with the basic mathematical concepts for graphical transformations. The lesson's objective was to teach students to recognize what type of transformation had taken place and describe the transformation based on the graph. I drew several example graphs on anchor chart paper and hung them all around the room to prepare the lesson. Typically, I would have labeled each point and anchor chart with the type of transformation and the formula for the algebraic rule it represents. However, for this lesson, I expected open-ended responses to facilitate students thinking differently. The students' first task was to engage in a gallery walk and write down their observations about each of the graphs and predict what type of transformation they believed each poster represented. I mentioned earlier that a significant component of the teacher's role in implementing an inquiry-based learning approach is to monitor and address misconceptions—meaning that we must be able to anticipate mistakes and guide students back on the correct path. The key to that is not stepping in to add new information or correct misconceptions too early. There were many disagreements between the students when they first began making observations. After allowing their conversations to simmer and meet an impasse, I introduced new guiding questions to help them dig deeper into the details.

A lesson that implements inquiry-based learning is a lesson that values productive struggle. During this lesson, I witnessed students having dialogue and correcting one another. If we genuinely desire to facilitate authentic student engagement, then those are the types of conversations you want to hear from students as they work.

INVESTIGATION, CONCLUSION, & DISCUSSION

Once students finished recording their observations and writing their final individual predictions, it was time to investigate and solve. Students created their solutions individually for each anchor chart, transitioning from one anchor chart to another when they heard me play music on the speaker. By the end of the lesson, students knew that they must show all of their work and determine which type of transformation was being displayed to have a fully completed assignment. While students were conducting their investigation and drawing conclusions, I made sure that I monitored their progress by walking around and noting students who should share their work with the class as an exemplar for each of the questions. I asked different students to share their conclusions with the class. It was so cool to see students asking each other why they made certain decisions and helping one another cement the learning for the day.

Inquiry-based learning is a concept that most educators associate with mathematics and science, but it is a framework that can be applied to any subject or grade level. For example, suppose a history class had a unit on the types of government. In that case, students could experiment with making decisions about the classroom using the guidelines for each government type. They could then talk about the pros and cons of each type of government. How much better do you think students might retain the kinds of government this way versus being told to memorize and regurgitate the definitions from a flashcard? I would be willing to bet the difference is significant. Inquiry-based learning gives students a genuine opportunity to build skills that will support their academic careers and live beyond it and prepare them for a productive life (Kaplan, 2019; Schmid and Bogner, 2015).

BENEFITS OF INQUIRY BASED LEARNING

- Inquiry-Based Learning is an Opportunity for Authentic Assessment
- Students Achieve and Demonstrate Mastery
- Inquiry-Based Learning Promotes Teamwork
- Inquiry-Based Learning Improves Knowledge Retention
- Student Interests Drive Inquiry-Based Learning

ENERGY & PACE, PHYSICAL MOVEMENT, AND MULTIMEDIA

One of the best ways to reduce, and potentially eliminate, stress as an educator is to "control the controllables" consistently. A big controllable for educators is our energy. We have the potential to add energy—no pun intended—or suck the energy out of a room. Let's put it this way; if educators are the thermostat, then students are the thermometers; they adapt to the temperature we set as leaders of the classroom. I cannot say enough how important it is that we monitor our energy. It is infectious. There are many ways of boosting the energy in your classroom: pacing, facial expressions, voice/tone, attitude, use of competition, etc.

Arguably, the most important of these is the pace at which your lesson is delivered. Keeping your lessons at a brisk pace will keep students bubbling over with anticipation for the next portion of the lesson. There are times that the lesson should slow down (i.e., reflection activities, independent work, during a model), and there are instances where the pace should increase (i.e., during competitions, group assignments, etc.) Educators should use pacing as a facilitation tool. It allows the educator to control the tempo and maximize the entire class time.

> **Energy & Pace**: The culturally responsive educator utilizes their body, voice, and facial gestures as teaching instruments to maintain a brisk pace. Teacher models a positive attitude and frequently embeds elements of playfulness and competition into the learning

Energy and communication go hand in hand for an educator, and with most of the communication being nonverbal, I needed to be intentional about my facial expressions and the tone of voice that I chose to address the students with—and it could change throughout the lesson. The goal is to change the pace throughout the lesson enough to keep the students' attention. The difference between starting a school day with a smile, handshake, and a mention of their name versus a frown and head nod could be significant for students not just in that moment to start the day, but for the stories they may be creating in their heads about how you view them. Let me ask you a question—if I were to ask your students how they think you view them, what might they say? If your answer is not positive, you may want to make an energy adjustment.

> **Physical Movement:** The culturally responsive educator implements active engagement strategies to keep students physically and psychologically involved. The teacher uses physical activities to stimulate learning or interest.

Ironically, this chapter is all about authentic student engagement because, in most classrooms, engagement is not valued above compliance. In most classrooms, I would venture to say that students are expected to stay in their seats, remain relatively quiet, and perform their tasks and action items individually. Well, my classroom was the complete opposite. The physical student movement was a key pillar of my success. We started each day with students standing on their chairs engaging in a call and response mantra led by another student leader. We did not stop there, though. I also planned different opportunities for students to move during the lesson physically. Students knew that at any moment, they could get up to use our interactive word wall. Our words for the week would be posted, and they could pull out the paper strip to see the definitions of each word and some examples. In addition, I taught math, so a significant component of my teaching included anchor charts to help remind students of key points about a given topic. I would hang them in different classroom areas, and they automatically had permission to use the anchor charts or even move to get a better view of the visual. Moving around the classroom gave students more ownership of their space, which led to even more engagement with the class and lessons.

> **Multimedia & Technology**: The culturally responsive educator complements the traditional curriculum with multimedia (examples, newspaper clippings, articles, song lyrics, plays, comics, video games, images, etc.) to spark student interest and curiosity. The teacher provides opportunities for students to utilize technology as a medium to facilitate and demonstrate learning.

All in all, we must keep in mind how our students learn the best and incorporate those elements of it into our practice. This current generation of students in our K–12 classrooms has never lived without the internet, YouTube, and instant access to information. Therefore, multimedia and technology should play a role in their understanding and development of content knowledge. Regardless of the content that we teach, there are countless ways to help students connect to things they are already interested in. You will learn student interests over time, but a straightforward way to accomplish that goal early is by giving your students an interests or hobby survey to start the school year. Collecting the data at the beginning of the school year made it easier for me to internalize their interests and find connection points along the way in my content. One example that I remember pretty vividly came while I was teaching the students about simple interest. Before introducing them to the computations, I wanted to help them understand the topic conceptually, so I showed a clip of a movie that they all had seen: *Barbershop*. The 5-minute clip showed Ice Cube's main character trying to repurchase his family barbershop from a loan shark. He had sold the barbershop to the shark for $20,000, and now the shark was charging him $40,000 to back out of the deal. After the movie clip was over, we discussed as a class why the payment to get the shop back was more than what he originally sold it for. Eventually, the students learned that the extra $20,000 is called interest. I could have given them the definition to start with, but instead, I chose to bring in an element of media to make my point clearer.

> Sometimes the best person for students to learn from is not their teacher. Maybe it is a peer. Perhaps it is song lyrics or a movie clip. Find what makes sense for your students, and do not hesitate to implement it into your instruction.

DIFFERENTIATION & RIGOR

In the ever-changing school landscape, certain things remain constant, like the need for differentiation and rigor. I know what you must be thinking, "Here we go talking about rigor again. . ." and I get it. Differentiation and rigor are some of the most crucial standards of authentic engagement. When I think about rigor and differentiation, I think about access. In other words, can every single student in my class cognitively access the lesson and the content?

> **Differentiation & Rigor:** The culturally responsive educator scaffolds the learning from basic to higher order thinking to activate prior knowledge, connect with students of various learning preferences, and support all students to produce high quality work and solve complex issues

Classrooms are meant to be places where students can thrive regardless of their skill level. Educators should get creative as they learn differentiation strategies. The first step of learning to differentiate well is to know students' strengths and weaknesses concerning the content being taught. Not only should the teacher know and be aware of student strengths and weaknesses, but the students should also learn to articulate their strengths and weaknesses for them-selves. I found that building students' investment into their data and schoolwork created a desire to improve. In addition, I would provide students with a choice day on certain Fridays throughout the year. It was a day where I prepared multiple activities on a select few standards that students could use to access additional practice. I gave the students some choice in the assignment that they completed, like a personal pathway, if you will. Based on the data students were tracking for themselves in their folders, they could articulate to me which path, or assignment, would be the highest leverage for them to complete. The element of choice could also provide what I call mild, medium, and spicy assignment options for students to choose from. I used this strategy if there is one standard or topic that all students in the class could use extra practice with. The mild, medium, and spicy options correlated with levels of difficulty on the assignment. This strategy gave students a new perspective on what they thought they could accomplish because they could now see their progression in understanding from the mild to the spicy assignment.

Another place where differentiation and rigor could be a focal point is with our questioning. Just like we prepare our assignments to increase from basic to higher-order thinking, our questioning should do the same throughout the lesson. To begin the lesson, questions should be designed to activate students' prior knowledge of the topic. Still, as we move deeper into the lesson, the questions should become a bit more abstract and capture evidence of student understanding. Start with the basic questions and ask yourself, "Would my struggling student be able to access the learning through this question?" Then transition to the more abstract questions and ask yourself, "Would this question challenge my high-achieving students?" If the answer to either of those questions is no, then some adjustments need to be made to ensure that the answer would be a resounding "YES!" Questions are only as good as the answers that follow them, which teachers should actively listen to to ask the next thought-provoking question. Questioning follows this cycle repeatedly throughout a lesson focused on differentiation and rigor. Ultimately, students should be challenged to explore solutions to complex problems—implementing differentiation and rigor strategies into your practice opens the door for all students to engage and participate (Mckinley, 2010). They may not all have the same starting point, but the end destination is the same.

MEANINGFUL EXPERIENCES

School plays a part in helping students discover and unearth meaning and purpose for their lives. If that statement is true, how well would you say your classroom or lessons help in that process? When I think about meaning and purpose, I am reminded that contributions beyond themselves drive most students. As a result, I often asked myself how my class can be the catalyst for students to understand their power and influence in the world indeed. It turns out that in my experience, the most meaningful experiences for students are those that extend beyond the four classroom walls.

> **Meaningful Experiences:** The culturally responsive educator plans purposeful experiences that allow students to role play, problem solve, and interact with one another in unique ways. Teacher designs activities that encourage students to create multicultural songs, dances, performances, and presentations.

A few years ago, Betsy DeVos, the Secretary of Education for the United States of America, visited the public school I was teaching at. We got little explanation as to why she was coming, but it was interesting to see the students' reaction to her visit. Whether we acknowledge it or not, our students have access to instant information via their computers and phones, and as such, they also have opinions about the world around them. During this visit, I saw students being empowered to share those opinions not just with their peers but with the world. An 8th Grade English Language Arts and Reading teacher at the school had an excellent idea for students to share their definitions of leadership via Facebook Live and YouTube in honor of Ms. DeVos's visit. Students were given

- Context of Ms. DeVos's decision-making as Secretary of Education, including diverse perspectives
- A framework to create their definitions of leadership
- A waiver for parents to give permission for their students to participate in the recording

Once each student gathered their ideas and thoughts, the teacher went live, and one by one, students began to share what leadership means to them and highlighting examples and non-examples from Ms. DeVos. We might not even know the long-term impact that this assignment may have had on those students, but I do know that each of them felt heard like never before on that day. I also know that some of those students overcame their fear of public speaking after this learning experience. Bottom line—meaningful experiences have long-lasting effects on our students' confidence and self-esteem. Push yourself beyond the content and ask yourself the same question: "How can my class be the catalyst for students to understand their power and influence in the world?" The answer may unlock a more significant meaning behind your class.

SUMMARY

Authentic engagement is about more than just following the rules or the structure of a lesson. It is about that spark that piques your students' interest and makes them want to be a part of the lesson. It is about tapping into those cultural funds of knowledge where the teacher is invested in defining authenticity for their students. Whether it is something as simple as the welcome rituals entering the classroom to civic engagement where students can see the change that they are making in the world around them, authentic engagement permits students to activate their internal motivation to work together for a common interest within the classroom. Too often, mainly, students of color are told to be quiet, sit down, walk in a straight line, to not speak too loudly, and not step out of what is expected to be the fixed structure of compliance in the classroom. Now, don't get me wrong, we all need routines and systems in the classroom for their highest functionality. However, the way we involve students in developing this structure by elevating student choice and voice is the critical component of authentic engagement. As educators, we must share the power in the classroom. We must share the leadership. We must share the ownership, and lastly, we must share that responsibility. It is not all about us. It is about the genuine investment we can build within each of our students by centering their backgrounds, hopes, dreams, experiences, and opportunities that they could not even fathom. As the chapter outlined, without omitting the academic rigor of the lesson to challenge our students using their critical thinking skills, there are several ways that we can find that balance in the classroom between meaningful engagement and academic achievement through multimedia and technology, energy, and pacing, differentiation, physical movement, inquiry-based learning, and as vital, shared evaluation. If we value receiving student feedback as much as we value giving it, I believe the classroom would be a better place for all students.

REFLECTION QUESTIONS

Take some time to reflect and make a plan for **Authentic Engagement** in your classroom using the guiding questions below:

1. What activities or inquiry-based learning opportunities have you planned to authentically engage your students?

2. How often do you allow students to evaluate the effectiveness of their lessons?

3. How do you plan to incorporate multimedia and technology to enhance the learning experience in your classroom?

4. What opportunities can you create that emphasizes student collaboration and discourse?

SOCIAL JUSTICE
CURRICULUM

SHONTORIA WALKER, ED.D.

> *Education is the most powerful weapon which you can use to change the world.*
>
> —*Nelson Mandela*

As an educator, I often took it upon myself to give my students what I believed I lacked most of my schooling experience. Growing up in a low-income community, single-parent home, and attending traditional public schools, I had not become aware of the inequities in education until I was exposed to

an African American studies course in college. I did not know that there were books by authors that taught me about who I truly am, where I come from, and the impact of oppressive historical systems in education and beyond. In grade school, we learned about significant figures critical to socio-political movements who had strong leadership character-istics like Dr. Martin Luther King Jr., but there was no mention of the influential impact of Minister Malcolm X. We learned about the resilient women of the Civil Rights Movement such as Rosa Parks, but I never learned of other powerful pioneers like Ms. Claudette Colvin, who is still alive today. If questioning the world around us was not already instilled within our upbringing, we were not nec-essarily taught how to think critically about society and search for meaning in the answers provided to us in the traditional school settings. Knowing that there were entire literary collections out there that I was not exposed to, made me ache for our students who are consistently denied this right to exposure throughout their educational careers. Although many teachers may argue that Social Jus-tice has no place in K–12th grade level curriculum and instruction, I believe in taking a slightly different approach. Social Justice should be embedded in our everyday instruction where societal issues are often highlighted so students can learn how to become agents of change that learn how to combat disparities, from health to education to politics to communities and schools; to make this world a better place for each and every one of us.

Education should be a vehicle where students can explore their cultural, racial, and ethnic identity; are enlightened by the world around them, given an opportunity to have their voices elevated louder than the educator in the room and the walls of the classroom; inspiring the ones that came before them. The world is the way it is today because, in their respective periods, young minds sparked movements that have transcended generations. Social Justice is not about forcing our personal beliefs, values, and philosophy upon our students based on our own experiences but providing them with the resources and tools to develop their own beliefs, values, and philosophies based on their own experiences. Providing students with the power to reach into the toolbox of their reality and say, "Oh, so that is why this is happening this way" or "Now I know how to create change."

As you explore the Social Justice Curriculum Domain in this chapter, I would like for you to take a step back and ask yourself how can I mentor the minds of students to inspire the next Mahatma Gandhi, Nelson Mandela, Muhammad

Ali, Socrates, Desmond Tutu, Susan B. Anthony, Dalai Lama, Ida B. Wells, Malala Yousafzai, Senator John Lewis, and countless others who sparked change to create the dynamic world we live in today.

Now that I have become Dr. Walker, I often look back on my educational experiences to determine at what points did a teacher who stood in front of me inspired me to continue pursuing my dreams? I've always wanted to become a doctor since I was nine years old. However, I never knew what field I wanted to enter or what steps it would take to accomplish my lifelong dream. The moments I felt that I most belonged to the school environment were during class discussions on interesting topics. When I was allowed to share my opinion or speak up, I remember lighting up as bright as a light bulb. Not because I simply wanted to talk, but because I always felt I had something to say, and too often, we were stifled in sharing our opinions in many of my classes. The majority of my traditional K–12th grade experience was saturated with the rules of silence and conformity. I remember whenever we were allowed to speak in our classroom and hear from our peers, I would always say out loud, "wow, I never knew that about you," or "I learned something new today." Knowing that I was going to be taught the skills necessary to pass the state or district assessments was something I expected from my classroom experience, however, when we were able to challenge some of the ideologies we were presented with and disrupt our thought patterns, there was a new spark—that something that I looked forward to every classroom experience. In these moments, I felt like my teachers were listening. I felt like my peers were listening. I felt like I was learning how to listen to myself. As a student, I felt as if my voice was lifted in the classroom. Providing that experience to the students that I have taught and something that you, as an educator, could do as well is what this domain is about.

Social Justice Curriculum Domain refers to the selected curriculum materials and resources in classroom instruction that creates a space for students to discuss the histories of oppression and inequalities while analyzing current injustices in our society. This domain aims to help students reflect on their lived experiences, explore social issues, and become social change agents. To truly address the components of this Social Justice Curriculum domain, a community must be built within the classroom where students are allowed to question and openly discuss the information presented to them. Social Movements are the fabric of American history and students should consistently have the opportunity to examine and deepen their understanding. Within this domain, culturally responsive educators will allow students to conduct in-depth exploration of concepts such as understanding inequity, self-concept, student agency, content relevance, anti-bias themes, diverse perspectives, cultural knowledge, and social action. As a result, students will not only be able to engage in an authentic examination of the world around them but stir impactful and lasting, positive change in society. Therefore, this chapter documents a Social Justice project that encompasses various lessons taught in my classroom. This project was grounded in the Education PowerED Culturally Responsive Teaching Domain 4: Social Justice Curriculum standards that I believe impacted the trajectory of many of my student's lives. This project was derived from their curiosity about policy, laws, and national social movements that directly or indirectly affected them. As an educator, you may choose to teach it differently, but the most crucial part is that you teach it.

SELF-CONCEPT

> **Self-Concept:** The culturally responsive educator reinforces positive attributes of students' identity and focuses on students' values, feelings, and beliefs about themselves. Teacher engages in discussion about how self-concept is influenced by students' sociopolitical context (Individual, Collective, Institutional, and Ideological).

When I first began my career in the field of education, I was afforded the unique opportunity of teaching in the community where I was raised at an all-boys academy. I desired to create encouraging spaces for my students to share their values, feelings, and, more specifically, their plight of being young men in society. I tasked myself with bringing a different approach to the learning environment by allowing the students to bring their lived experiences and community into the classroom once I was informed that I was the first educator to teach at the school who had grown up in the surrounding neighborhood. I designed sessions called "Real Talk Fridays" to intentionally create this space for the young men in my classroom and any others who desired to join. As things were happening globally, students would come to school with questions about the impact of societal decisions such as the presidential elections or community policing or issues that affected the community directly. For example, one student questioned why there was only one local grocery food store that did not focus on healthier food choices like other larger food chains in more affluent neighborhoods. As students entered my classroom with various questions, I noticed there was a gap in students' background knowledge about the issues that they brought forth. They didn't understand economic disadvantages of communities of color, or health disparities, or inequitable access to better food choices, or even the difference between councilmen and councilwomen versus State Representatives. Because I did not want to deter from instructional time, I presented an idea to the administration about providing students with an opportunity to discuss these pressing issues as an entire peer group to learn and explore critical concepts together. The administrative team was highly supportive and even offered their resources by expanding the program once we had a strong understanding of the need for such space. They would assist with bringing in a network of influential individuals such as football players, poets, and local civic leaders to provide the students with additional perspective and insight on the topics at hand.

"Real Talk Fridays" was born. On Friday mornings, beginning at 7:30 am, the young men of the school would file into the designated classroom and be encouraged to bring their authentic selves. It was meant as a moment of solidarity; a newly formed community; a shared space of vulnerability and understanding. Students would greet one another with fist bumps and secret handshakes that signaled a meeting of the minds, that "we are in this together." For those who may have felt like an outcast throughout the school day, Friday mornings were meant as a zone of belonging. We would start with our daily affirmation, adopted from a viral educator video, modified to fit the needs and circumstances of the students I served. It would signal our beginning. I would open by posing a question in which all students were expected to respond to in unison. It went a little like this:

TEACHER: What if it's too tough?
STUDENTS: I'm going to push through!
TEACHER: What if you're just too young?
STUDENTS: That's not true!
TEACHER: What if you're not good enough?
STUDENTS: That's not true!
TEACHER: Why?
STUDENTS: Because I can do anything I put my mind to!
TEACHER: I believe in you!
STUDENTS: Chin up!
TEACHER: Believe in yourself.
STUDENTS: Head High!

Teacher:	Why?	
Students:	Because I can do anything I put my mind to!	

The sense of community built from this simple affirmation allowed the students to feel connected to the energy, their peers, and the learning environment. Any student that may have walked into my room that had a bad night of sleep or were yelled at by a parent that morning or with bits of self-doubt and may have suffered from imposter syndrome was reminded that their strengths, not their weaknesses, will be uplifted in this community space with others who may or may not share their plight. However, we would seek to understand one another's circumstances and approach our conversations with perspective and empathy. There is no way we could have had conversations as student-centered as "Real Talk Fridays" without first ensuring that students were mindful of their values and belief in self; to be confident enough to share their true feelings and opinions on a given topic, especially if it was something that mirrored their reality or hit close to home.

A guide that I would use to plan for "Real Talk Fridays" is below:

Current Event (Time, Date, National or Global Impact)	Background Knowledge to Build Insight	Anticipated Misconceptions

Students were able to provide input on the given topics of the week by placing anonymous questions or recommendations in our "Suggestion" bucket throughout the week located near the door of the classroom. Students would bring in questions, topics, or themes based on the things they may have seen on the television or in the community that may have directly or indirectly impacted them or their way of being. To foster deep discussions where the students would bring their personal experiences into the classroom, I was sure to provide them with a brief reading to build background knowledge or schema to build insight about the chosen topic of the week. Therefore, when we explored various issues in society, students were able to have at least some type of reference or piece of texts that would support building background knowledge, just in case, some young men may not have been as knowledgeable about the given topic. In this way, we built a multilayered understanding of the individual, collective, institutional, and ideological based on a small stint of curiosity. It also provided students with a sense of ownership of their learning. Although we had to learn the embedded standards within the curriculum during our core English Language Arts instructional time, this was an additional slot of time set aside that further piqued student interest. This allowed me to level the gap in my classroom and encouraged those who may have initially remained silent to speak up. Anticipating student misconceptions, just as we may do for our core content classes, allowed me to be prepared to answer any questions my students may have about the given topic. The value in this is that I could plan for my response to ensure that my potential bias did not influence my students' thoughts or actions about the topic. Although the administration did not require lesson plans for our sessions, I still took the time to plan and prepare for the sessions with the students.

One of my most vivid memories of "Real Talk Fridays" was when students began to question the cases that sparked national outrage of the unfortunate killing of young men such as Michael Brown, Trayvon Martin, and Oscar Grant. In August of 2014, 18-year-old Michael Brown was fatally shot by a police officer in Ferguson, Missouri. These cases consumed the media, and I noticed that many of the young men would enter the classroom juxtaposing their reality with what they heard in the media. During a "Real Talk Fridays" session, one student explained how he walked home every day from our neighborhood stores just like Michael Brown, so he could only imagine how scared Brown must have felt when the cops pulled up. The same as Trayvon Martin when he was walking home. "You just gotta do enough to survive and hope you make it back home," one student replied. Students debated on whether to run, whether to stop, whether to scream, or whether to simply stand there. Another student who had a very different experience with law enforcement could not understand why the young men who were close in age couldn't just be taken to jail. "Why did they have to be killed?" Other students questioned how protesting could possibly change the fatal outcomes.

The following week, the young men would enter with a myriad of additional questions about another similar case, young Trayvon Martin. It seemed as if they could not move past the facts of the case and demanded an extension of the conversation to gain a deeper understanding.

- "Well, I wear a hoodie every single day, am I considered suspicious?"
- "How could George Zimmerman not know he was just a kid?"
- "I'm just as tall as him, do you think people see me as an adult too?"
- "I usually stay at my grandmother's house in Georgia; now I gotta be extra careful because I don't want people to think I'm there to rob or steal when I'm only visiting."
- "Why are they trying to figure out who did what when Trayvon is dead?"

The facts are that Trayvon Martin's killing happened on a rainy night on February 26, 2012, in Sanford, Florida. The case sparked national outrage as many did not understand how a neighborhood guard could unjustifiably kill a 17-year-old Black teenager walking home from a convenience store after purchasing a can of iced tea and a bag of Skittles. According to reports, he was perceived as suspicious due to wearing a black hoodie and walking in a strange neighborhood. Reports would later reveal that young Trayvon Martin was visiting with his father and stepmom for a short time away from his permanent home, where he resided with his mother and older brother.

UNDERSTANDING INEQUITY

> **Understanding Inequity:** The culturally responsive educator equips students with the knowledge and understanding of the history of inequality and oppression. The teacher helps students recognize inequity due to human-created social and economic relations that can be challenged.

As an educator, I would have to take a logical approach to the questions that arose from my students. Although I had lived experiences of inequities and systemic oppression, I chose to give the students the tools to learn and dissect the written, audio, and media of the Trayvon Martin case for themselves and arrive at their own conclusion. As educators, that should always be where we stand when teaching Social Justice. Our students are fountains that consume a wealth of material every single day. Nonetheless, for them to be true agents of change, students must be able to use the given information and decide how to act upon it.

By this time, we had completed the district and state-mandated assessments so our sole focus could be on this project-based learning task in alignment with the state standards. I chose to use student curiosity to teach Debate and Public Speaking for the final six weeks of school. The culminating project, approved by administration and supported by all teachers at the campus, was that students would conduct a mock trial in moot court at Thurgood Marshall School of Law at the Historically Black College/University, Texas Southern University in Houston, Texas. I crafted this project with students because I knew first-hand that many of them did not understand law, policy, or the sequence of events leading up to the Trayvon Martin incident. Many of them did not understand why nationwide movements and national outrage were created after unjust killings of Black men.

Unfortunately, many of their lived experiences did not include being in a courtroom on the "right" side of the law. During "Real Talk Fridays," students would speak from personal experiences about how their uncles or brothers or fathers had many disheartening encounters with law enforcement or were currently in prison. With this in mind, I desired to craft a very specific learning experience where students could walk away having the tools and resources to either seek out more information or now have a better understanding of why their family member, friend, or even those who they did not know personally have varying encounters, positive and negative, with law enforcement. In my selfish desire, I hoped that a deeper understanding of policies and laws would, in turn, possibly save their lives. Until this day, I cannot guarantee that this project changed every single student's perception of social movements. Yet, I can say that I thoroughly planned with my team of teacher leaders in Science, Social Studies, Art, and Math to create an unparalleled learning experience.

"Real Talk Fridays" allowed for open discussion where students could share in a structured manner their feelings and emotions. Their passion was always there, but I noticed that there was often a gap in knowledge, a deep understanding of systems. For example, the "Stand Your Ground" law used as the justified reason in the Trayvon Martin and George Zimmerman case. Students also lacked the knowledge of the political system, beyond the foundation of skills taught in their Social Studies class, such as policing in communities of color.

CULTURAL KNOWLEDGE AND CONTENT RELEVANCE

> **Cultural Knowledge:** The culturally responsive educator selects curriculum materials where students explore various cultures and groups through artifacts, history, etc. Students gain an authentic knowledge of different ethnic groups and an appreciation of diversity.

> **Content Relevance:** The culturally responsive educator provides curriculum materials on social, economic, and political issues related to ethnicity, gender, and exceptionality. Teacher plans learning encounters that validate students' lived realities, cultural identities, and heritage.

We would first start our Debate unit by exploring the intricacies of interlocking systems from the educational system to policing in America, the school to prison pipeline, and what would true police reform accomplish by analyzing the Oscar Grant case. I believed this was a great start because this case was similar to the ones the students had questions about. Oscar Grant was a 22-year-old Black man killed by police officers in a BART Train Station in Oakland, California. *Fruitvale Station* (2013) was a movie that detailed the day in the life of Oscar Grant leading up to his killing. Once this movie was released, much of the media began to bring to light the numerous killings of young Black men at the hands of law enforcement. A classroom guide created by the San Francisco Film Society was a great resource in teaching the film to understand why Oscar Grant was killed and turn films such as these into meaningful learning experiences for students. The lessons could be transferred across disciplines outside of English Language Arts such as Art, History, Social Studies, and those who would prefer an even broader understanding, Legal Studies. I designed the lesson in this way because I did not want students' knowledge and skills to only be tied to and housed in the English Language Arts classroom. Students would be able to transfer these skills in other classes to continue to seek further connections to the learning.

Additionally, I wanted students to look beyond the vocabulary terms used during our lessons. In not simply finding the definition, but knowing what it means to be an **activist** and practice **activism**; what are our **Civil Rights** and how have we fought to keep them over time; what does it mean to lead with **Compassion**; is **Family** only those who are biological to us or can this word be used in a broader sense; who are those who have benefited from the **Justice** system and those who have possibly profited from it; what about those who have been denied justice; how does the **law** protect you and me; what are the contributing factors of **Police Violence** and looking beyond it; what is needed to end it; as well as what are the constructs of **Race** and **Racism**.

ANTI-BIAS THEMES

> **Anti-Bias Themes:** The culturally responsive educator structures learning to allow for deep exploration of anti-bias themes. Teacher models how to identify, interpret, and speak out against bias.

It was imperative that my students considered all sides of each story shown in the media, in newspapers, on social media, etc., when analyzing critical stories that sparked national outrage. Students need to recognize their own bias and how it may influence their viewpoint while also recognizing the bias presented in these varying stories. As you can imagine, my students did not first fully identify the bias they brought to the "Real Talk Fridays" discussions when these critical conversations were presented. I noticed that their perspectives of the unfortunate killings often resulted in students pulling from their own negative experiences and encounters with law enforcement. Recurrently, students' immediate reactions would be hurt, pain, and resentment, while they would recount alternative ways the police encounters could have been carried out to save young lives.

Unfortunately, when conversations such as these are carried out in the classroom, educators often believe that we cannot foster healthy discussions because it is thought that we are forcing our personal opinions upon the students. As educators, we must also recognize our own bias and be in tune with how that may impact student learning in the ways that they may respond. Students must know that we care about the material presented. Their voice is the main voice that is raised throughout the learning. More often than not, our students' biases stem from their family, their community, and their environment, which may be vastly different from peer to peer. Therefore, when I taught the foundational skills of Speech and Debate to prepare for the mock trial, I wanted my students to learn how to authentically speak with clarity, even if it involved using their native tongue. In the beginning, I noticed that many of my students were shy to speak up and hesitant to present in front of their peers. Many would think that it may have been their age. However, when I allowed the students to talk through their fears, I found that they mimicked negative stereotypes stemming from biases that they heard over time, whether from school, community, society, or the media.

On the one hand, some of the young men felt that if their speech did not align to the standards of whiteness, they must remain silent; they had nothing to say. On the other hand, when we were learning the techniques of debate, many of the students were apprehensive about speaking on topics that they may have been interested in but chose to remain mum because they were afraid that they lacked the background knowledge and full context to talk about the issue. This was heartbreaking to me. It makes me think of how our great orators, such as Fred Hampton, who at the young age of 19, led socio-political movements that changed an entire generation. It makes me think of Frederick Douglass, who, I'm sure, took the time to learn how to move the masses. What if these two and countless other dominating figures never learned Speech and Debate. What if they were never exposed? Once I got my students confident with the foundational skills of Speech and Debate, they could not be stopped. Therefore, when the biases arose during our debates of specific topics, students now had the tools and skills to challenge those thoughts in healthy discussions. The purpose was to seek understanding, to seek knowledge, to learn from not just me, as the educator, but to learn from their peers.

I was able to leverage the media as a critical resource in my lessons as well. I think of fireside chats used during The Great Depression, newspaper articles and press that chronicled historical moments used as primary sources of information where young changemakers are galvanized to join movements. Therefore, I placed various stations around my classroom for students to see, hear and read about archival shifts. Each station had the same thematic focus. At one station, students were able to listen to podcasts; at another, students watched YouTube videos, and at the third station, students viewed *Time* magazine covers that marked these movements while also reading brief articles about these significant events. Therefore, beyond learning Speech and Debate, students were exposed to and taught how to analyze moments where the classroom was transformed into a walking gallery, a museum of movements.

For students, this generated more questions about policy and law and the bias that may lie in how many of these cases have been decided. They were also interested in how these cases may have generated new laws and policies as a result of the unfortunate deaths. For example, the Sandra Bland Act in Texas that mandates that county jails must now divert individuals with substance abuse and mental health issues toward treatment as well as requires that jail deaths be investigated by independent law enforcement agencies. Repealing of the controversial Stand Your Ground Law that states that individuals have the right to use deadly force to protect themselves against an intruder in which George Zimmerman was able to claim to justify the killing of young Martin. Even thinking about transformative policy laws today, such as the George Floyd Policing Act of 2020, which would establish a framework that would prevent racial profiling by law enforcement at the local, state, and federal levels. Furthermore, understanding the difference between first, second, and third-degree convictions of suspects to become more knowledgeable about how the system works and allow the students to decide whether it is working for them or against them. While also having the choice in dedicating their time as they grow older to influence policy and create meaningful change in their communities.

DIVERSE PERSPECTIVES

Diverse Perspectives: The culturally responsive educator uses curriculum materials that describe historical, social, and political events from a wide range of racial, ethnic, cultural, and language perspectives. Teacher encourages students to develop multicultural perspectives that respect the dignity and worth of all people.

At this point, students had generated interest in cases that sparked national social justice movements, discussed in an open forum called "Real Talk Fridays" about their thoughts and opinions on the matter and how it impacts them mentally and emotionally as young men of color in society. They also learned speech, debate, and policy that was pivotal for these cases. As we continued to prepare for our mock trial, I wanted to ensure that not only students' voices were elevated, but their diverse perspectives were heard in a structured manner through formal discussions called Socratic Seminars. The seminars aimed to center student-generated questions to explore meaning, identity, and connection. Once a week leading up to the mock trial, I ensured that students continued the conversations with their new learning by sharing their perspectives from their unique backgrounds to encourage and promote multicultural awareness. The beauty of the community that I taught in was the mix of ethnicities, experiences, and realities that students brought into the classroom. Because it was a historical neighborhood, older families still populated much of the community. In what was once a majority Black neighborhood, compelled students to learn about the shifting demographics that made up the surrounding areas of the school.

I set up the Socratic Seminars in a way where I would arrange the chairs in circle formation, an inner circle, and an outer circle. This gave the inner circle of students the ability to discuss with a smaller subset of their peers and the outer circle of students to observe, listen, and provide feedback. Each round would last approximately 15 minutes, and then I would have the inner circle of students switch with the outer circle. This new group of students would have a new conversation on the same topic. It was a delight to see how the students would become excited when they entered the room and saw the desk arrangement as they looked forward to something different instead of the standard rows in the classroom. I believe it built a sense of awareness as we sat around the circle and took notice of the various hues and personalities that made up the conversation. Too often in the classroom, the teacher is the center of the room, and students do not get the opportunity to literally face each other and speak to one another in a structured format. The Socratic Seminar gave each individual student an opportunity to not only be heard, but to be seen.

It was at these moments that I believe students indeed noticed the diversity of input that was in that encouraging space created for them. I also noticed that the Socratic Seminar lowered students' inhibitions and hesitancy to speak. The format of the discussion allowed for a collective thought. I always stood on the outside of both circles in a manner that disrupted the traditional student sit-and-lecture style of learning by ensuring that I was only the facilitator through this learning experience. As the discussion proceeded, students in the outer circle were expected to provide feedback on the following questions:

Feedback Questions for Socratic Seminar

- Did my peers arrive at a reasonable conclusion about the topic?

- Were the speech and debate techniques learned in the previous lesson observed in this discussion?

- Did I hear accountable talk from my peers?

Creating this experience allowed the students to display their enthusiasm as they had never done before. Now, instead of asking me the questions about how George Zimmerman's bias may have played a role in young Trayvon Martin's killing, they were able to pose the question to their peers and support their answer with evidence using the background knowledge from the various pieces of literature and texts I provided them over time.

Speaking of literature, after the Socratic Seminar, I thought that the students should also have the ability to gather in an even smaller group and discuss specific pieces of literature in depth to explore all that it had to offer from a meta standpoint. With a guide, students were able to seek the answers by exploring similar themes in classical literature using poems from "America" by Walt Whitman, Langston Hughes "I, Too, Am America" and "Let America Be America Again." Students were given a choice in which set of poems they wanted to analyze with their group where they made texts to world connections to gain a larger sense of historical context in the case of young Trayvon Martin and others. Unlike the Socratic Seminar, where students had whole group discussions with the entire class, students were grouped in smaller groups of four and were required to take on roles such as the Scribe, the Challenger, the Devil's Advocate, and the Timekeeper.

Student Roles for Literature Circles	
Scribe	This student takes notes as the group discusses. This student prepares the worksheet or reports for presentation.
Challenger	This student seeks connections of the work by reflecting on the work. These students challenge the group to think deeper about the content of the work.
Devil's Advocate	This student ensures that the group avoids premature agreements about the work by making sure the group looks at all sides of the literature, argument, or work.
Timekeeper	This student keeps track of time to ensure that the group begins, ends on time, and does not stay too long on a given topic or section of the work.

I believe that no kid should leave our classrooms without this critical skill. Social Justice is not about gaslighting our youth to make them overturn the government or persuading them to think as I do. It is about providing our youth with learning experiences where they can learn about themselves and those who came before them who have made this a more equitable world for every one of us. It is about allowing our youth the space to inquire about the world around them.

Therefore, as we prepared for the moot court at Thurgood Marshall School of Law at Texas Southern University, students openly expressed their eagerness for tackling an issue they felt was near and dear to their hearts. They acknowledged that I listened and heard what they wanted to learn about in our "Real Talk Fridays" discussions and turned those questions into an authentic learning experience. Like many of his peers,

According to the Oxford Dictionary, the definitions of the terms "social" and "justice" are to connect with society and the fair treatment of people. I felt that when my students came to me with questions about their position in society based on what they have seen in the media; it was my responsibility to provide them with the tools, skills, resources, and knowledge to be able to decipher the information given to them, take ownership of their learning and choose to be agents of change.

one student spoke about this being his first opportunity in a courtroom for the "right" reasons. He discussed with his peers that his mother, father, and countless family members had been in and out of prison throughout his childhood. Therefore, his only association with a courtroom was for someone like him to show up in a prison suit with handcuffs to be sentenced to an extended amount of time behind bars. He could not even fathom the possibility of someone like himself being the Judge, the Bailiff, the Prosecutor, the Defense Attorney, or even practicing his civic duty as a juror on major or minor cases. Because he had been sold this nightmare, in my opinion, he had never thought of himself beyond being the prisoner in a courtroom. Can you imagine the detriment this has on our youth today? How many students are sitting in your classroom with this same exact perspective?

Without learning experiences such as these, how do we genuinely prepare our youth to face the world before them? As an educator, it was never just about teaching students the knowledge to get out or leave their community but giving them the power to positively impact their community; to enhance their learning experience beyond the classroom. Where the students could go back to those same family members and inform them as well; to encourage them to become the knowledge holder or the wise one to influence the next generation. That is what Social Justice is.

SOCIAL ACTION

Social Action: The culturally responsive educator constructs scenarios for students to practice social advocacy skills and utilize tools of activism to become effective change agents in the school and broader community. The teacher assigns activities that challenge students to examine their beliefs and engage in the struggle to make society more equitable.

On Friday, July 12, 2013, George Zimmerman was found not guilty on the charges of second-degree murder and manslaughter in the slaying of Trayvon Martin. In preparation for moot court, I brought in expert law school students to inform us about the details of the case. We studied witness accounts that could be found on public forums. We also watched the actual clips of the court case provided by YouTube. We analyzed press and articles released to the public. We combined everything we learned from Speech, Debate, the Socratic Seminar discussions, and Literature Circles to analyze all material necessary for the case. In addition, as a class, we held auditions for a student Judge, Bailiff, Jurors, Defense Attorney, and Prosecutor. Everyone else who was not an active participant in the case at moot court was the court audience. Their roles were to provide feedback to their peers, just as we did in the Socratic Seminar. Although we reviewed the evidence as an entire class to understand the elements of the case, the chosen prosecution and defense teams prepared for the mock trial in isolation from the whole class with other disciplinary teachers such as the Art teacher, Social Studies, Math, Science, Assistant Principal as well as the PE coach.

The entire school understood that an assignment of such magnitude would require all hands-on deck. In this way, the students were able to see how we worked together as a school team. For the field trip, each student was provided school funded courtroom notebooks, notepads, pens, and pencils. Students were asked to dress up in formal attire, suit, and tie. If they did not have access to these garments at home, we collected donated clothing from male teachers. When students saw each other dressed up, they complimented one another, gave each other personalized handshakes and high fives with deep smiles.

We rode a school bus to the Thurgood Marshall School of Law at Texas Southern University. Excitement filled the student's faces. I knew that the significance of this moment would stick with the students for the long term. Being able to carry out this actual project at such a historic institution such as Texas Southern University, one of the largest and comprehensive historical Black universities, where notable figures attended such as Barbara Jordan. A leader in the Civil Rights Movement and the first African American elected to the Texas Senate after Reconstruction. She was also the first African American woman elected to the United States House of Representatives. Jordan stated, "If the society today allows wrongs to go unchallenged, the impression is created that those wrongs have the approval of the majority." This project was not meant for students to conduct performative work as a result of them not liking the outcome of the George Zimmerman trial. It was because they did not fully understand the system that allowed him to walk free.

Once we arrived at the school of law, we were greeted by current male law school students and alumni who knew the administration of our school very well. The students were able to ask questions about their law school journey and their experiences. The law school students explained how they came from the communities that the students had come from. They also explained to the students that experiences such as these were why they decided to pursue law; in essence, to save themselves and inform those around them.

During the mock trial, I believed that the students embodied not only the rehearsed roles, but we were able to see on full display a compilation of all the skills and techniques they had been taught since we began this project-based learning experience. At one moment during the student defendant's closing arguments where he exclaimed that there was no reason why Trayvon Martin should be on trial because he was not physically present to defend himself, the student was brought to tears. The killing of the young man, who he declared resembled his brothers and his family members, was unjustified.

The emotion and intensity that exuded this young man was felt across the courtroom. Even the adults in the room were moved. This was not a part of the rehearsal, but I believe that in that moment, the student exhibited the epitome of what it meant to take ownership of his learning; beyond reading and comprehending but connecting to the case so profoundly. After closing arguments, the student jurors were led to the juror hall with another chaperone teacher. They were to discuss the evidence presented before them and determine George Zimmerman's fate. The chaperone reported back to me the gravity of the experience as students debated with their peers; a proper understanding of what was at stake.

A project of this magnitude was designed to allow students to connect the learning to their realities, their communities; to embody the power and resistance of civil icons, those who did not understand the world around them as well, but were determined to create change and impact. It was designed to empower students with what is needed to save their own lives or possibly their family. It was designed to provide a sense of inclusion. For far too long, students consume mounds of negative stereotypical information from the society that too often tells them that they do not belong; that they are not in charge of their fate; that they must only accept what is given to them and not challenge or think for themselves; that they must not walk in the footsteps of those who came before them because social justice is only for those who can afford to benefit from it and not for all.

AGENCY

> **Agency:** The culturally responsive educator encourages students to analyze the circumstances of their lived experience and develop practical tools to persevere through challenges stemming from social justice.

After the student jurors returned to the courtroom, proper court proceedings were carried out. The verdict of the case was reported, and we returned to the schoolhouse. We reconvened in the classroom just as we had done before during "Real Talk Fridays" discussions to debrief the students' experiences. Some of the students spoke about how they felt an uneasiness in their gut as they listened to their peers present the case because it reminded them of when they watched the actual case on television. One student recalled how he and his family broke down in tears when they heard the verdict live for the first time. Although this was only a mock trial, and he was well aware that we could never go back and change the sequence of events, he was hoping that maybe, just maybe, things would be different this time around. Another student spoke as he listened to the defense team defend young Trayvon Martin. He asserted that he could not help but think about young Martin's parents and older brother and how they must have felt as they sat in the audience and listened to the court proceedings. A student juror reported how now he understands how difficult it must be for jurors to make the right decision based on evidence despite public opinion and outcry. He stated, "Although the case may have made them feel a certain way, I learned that jurors must stay faithful to the law and the evidence presented before them. It is so important to listen carefully and be all in."

Another student spoke about how when we first started talking about the Trayvon Martin case, he did not know about the other similar cases, including the similarities between the brutal case of Emmett Till in 1955. He initially was infuriated because he simply could not understand why it kept happening over and over again. He explained that he refused to speak at moments during class discussions and thanked me for allowing him to simply listen over time. As he sat in the courtroom near the end of the mock trial, he expressed that he realized that this learning experience was not about despising a man like George Zimmerman because "that ain't gone get us nowhere," in his words. But it was about understanding how the system works, either for minority groups or against them, where, unfortunately, history continues to repeat itself. He now felt a deep urge to learn more so that he could do more. Many of the students spoke about the weight of the case. Another student expressed that he had never seen someone who looked like him in the judge chair or even thought that he could become a lawyer one day. Still, after an experience such as this, he believed that was the career he wanted to pursue. All students showed gratitude to the faculty and staff for listening to them and allowing them to be a part of a lesson such as this.

Though this was only one detailed account of teaching Social Justice grounded in the Culturally Responsive Social Justice standards, there are many other instances where I have continued to spiral in authentic learning experiences where students are the drivers of the lessons. In all facets of education, I have found that this is the key to closing the opportunity gap for students from marginalized communities. Once I recognized that many of my students operated solely from survival mode, because it had been a place I worked from as well, I knew that one way to keep them engaged and pique their interest was to allow them to bring their obstacles and their concerns to the classroom even if I only had these students for one academic school year.

In the year 2020, the George Floyd case triggered a massive social movement similar to other monumental moments in a time where all people, no matter race, creed, or religion, came together and raised their voices to demand change. Contrary to popular belief, this was not the first awakening of the masses. The difference with the George Floyd case was the power of social media.

For many that may be wondering, students also exceeded achievement expectations set forth by the district and the campus. I placed this at the end of this chapter because, for whatever reason, the education world believes that if we enrich the curriculum with opportunities such as this one, then our students will fail or lack the essential skills and knowledge necessary to pass the standardized testing and data checkpoints required by the campus, district, or state. However, I would urge educators to consider the opposite. Opportunities such as this one enhances the learning experience for all students. For those students who do not see their place in the curriculum or do not see themselves in the literature, who feel excluded or isolated from the classroom experience. As educators, we must believe that we are nurturing the next generation of changemakers. The classroom is where it starts.

SUMMARY

In this educational system, we must have a clear understanding of the inequities between economic and racial lines. Vernon A. Wall (2007) details myths about Social Justice that must be dispelled. Here are a few listed below.

- Myth #1: Social Justice has no real scholarly basis and is a vague concept.

- Myth #2: Social Justice is simply multiculturalism and diversity renamed.

- Myth #3: Discussing Social Justice moves us away from conversations on sexism, classism, and racism, etc.

- Myth #4: Social Justice focuses on action rather than personal work.

- Myth #5: Social Justice issues are not an interest of students.

- Myth #6: Only idealists with a liberal cause are the focus of Social Justice.

However, as you can see in this chapter, enriching the curriculum with Social Justice allows students to be involved in civic engagement to enhance the student experience within a classroom. When students have a deep understanding of the world around them, it allows them to impact their communities and neighborhoods; to make this world a better place for all. In this chapter, you were able to explore how the Social Justice Curriculum standards were embedded into the classroom that allowed the students to bring their authentic selves into the classroom; to question the world around them; to voice their concerns, opinions, and thoughts about the happenings in society. Although we may think the classroom is not a place for these conversations, it is as mentioned at the beginning of this chapter.

However, understanding your own bias first, and doing the initial work as the educator, is critical to doing this work. Teaching through a social justice lens empowers our students to be more than they could imagine.

> Students have diverse perspectives and diverse cultural backgrounds that add value to the classroom curriculum.

REFLECTION QUESTIONS

Take some time to reflect and make a plan for **Social Justice** in your classroom using the guiding questions below:

1. How well are you as an educator familiar with histories of oppression and inequality? What have you done to further equip yourself with this knowledge?

2. What learning opportunities have you created for your students to understand the histories of inequality?

3. How have you created a culture in your classroom for students to identify, interpret, and speak out against bias?

4. How have you been actively involved in social advocacy allowed for student agency inside and outside of your classroom?

CULTURALLY RESPONSIVE TEACHING: FROM THEORY TO PRACTICE

Education either functions as an instrument which is used to facilitate integration of the younger generation into the logic of the present system and bring about conformity, or it becomes the practice of freedom, the means by which students deal critically and creatively with reality and discover how to participate in the transformation of their world.
—*Paulo Friere, Pedagogy of the Oppressed*

Throughout this book, we have given you insight into our classroom instructional space while detailing how we interpreted the theory of culturally

responsive pedagogy and implemented the practice for our students. The focus was on the practice
of crafting meaningful learning experiences for students of color. Those that look like us and those that
do not. Students who may have spent their academic
journeys feeling isolated from the curriculum and
instruction year after year. Students who may have
felt lost or forgotten and even struggled to find the
connection and relevance to the texts. As educators,
we know that our students thrive in different environments. Therefore, it is our responsibility that we create that space for them to see success as attainable.

We hope that you notice some common themes throughout our personal and professional journeys to see how we
did it, as we anticipate that you will be able to recreate more
profound experiences for your students. When we began
teaching, we were not aware of the pathways we would lead
with our students. However, it is one that we truly appreciate
in our growth and development as four dynamic educators. As
first-year educators, when most were simply trying to survive,
find that work-life balance, and get through each day without
losing their heads, we saw the classroom as a place to spark
change. A place to live out our imagination. A place to elevate
student voice and student choice. We worked within the con-
straints and expectations of our respective educational institutions. But we created magic, where we felt there seemed
to be none—providing students with experiences that we

hope will stick with them for a lifetime. Take a moment to think back to something that happened in the classroom during your time as a student that was so profound that you can remember that same feeling today. What if we inundated our students with these experiences so much so that 10, 20, 30 years down the line, they don't simply recall a handful of experiences, but so many that they cannot even choose. Imagine that. That is what culturally responsive teaching and practice is all about. We have to do something different for our students to give them a chance at perspective, a chance at exploration, a chance at opportunity, a chance at life. Though we started by saying the educational system built to serve students of color is failing them, we now have the opportunity to revolutionize the educational experience for all. Let's stop placing a band-aid over an ever-bleeding wound and treat it at its core.

From the Black church, to the knowledge and skills built from a nurturing and caring parent, to classroom discussions that made us feel a sense of pride and belonging, we were sure to use our own schooling experiences as students of color to inform our work and desire to give our students more. Those experiences provided us with a clear sense of self in that particular moment. However, one of the most integral elements of our work is that we were clear about our positionality as educators at the center of the classroom. We were clear about our positionality in how our identity and potential bias influenced our outlook on the world. And yes, we also actually mean our physical position within our classrooms.

Think about when you walk into your classroom and greet your students. Where do you stand? Think about when you introduce the new material or the new concept of the day. Where do you stand? Think about when there is a whole group or even small group discussion within your classroom. Where do you stand or sit? Now think about the end of class, maybe the bell has rung, or the clock is signaling that it is time to transition to the next class. Where do you stand? Often, the teacher is the center of the classroom.

All eyes are focused in one direction. From day to day, students may enter their classrooms with their peers, but they do not get the opportunity to physically face them and look at them and talk to them because the educator is the center of the room. One of the most common themes throughout our narratives as educators in the classroom is that because students could perceive that the teacher holds all of the knowledge because they are at the center of the room the majority of the time, we literally took a step back out of the center, and placed students there elevating their capacity to lead in all facets; where each peer had an opportunity to share their knowledge and share the wealth of their cultural background. Our physical position in our classroom declared that the educator was also a student of the classroom. A learner amongst learners. We noticed that the students then began to seek knowledge not just from the teacher—increasing student ownership of learning, student confidence, and student responsibility.

This does not mean that the educator does not introduce the material or the content, in essence, where you have all the students' attention at moments during the classroom instruction. That is why we are all in this field; to provide students with the knowledge, skills, and tools to help them become contributing citizens in society. However, it does mean that 80 to 90 percent of the class time, the teacher acts as the facilitator of the learning. Think back to our classroom stories. If it was a gallery walk, the students kinesthetically moved around the classroom. At the same time, the teacher stepped back to observe the learning, the curiosity, or "aha" moments students may have had. If it was a Socratic Seminar, the teacher positioned themselves on the outside of the inner and outer circles to observe the rich discussion amongst peers. If it was a press conference in anticipation to speak with the former Secretary of Education, Ms. Betsy DeVos, while the students spoke as journalists and held the camera to stream live videos for their peers, the teacher physically stood back to allow the students to be the center of the learning for these experiences. Now, I will say for those who are not used to this level of autonomy for the students, there may be some hesitancy in controlling the urge not to be the center. Some of it could be personal, some of it could be you, as the educator, are fearful that the students would not grasp the learning without you. Dismally, it could be that resistance of giving up the power within the classroom. However, have you asked yourself why you are resistant to giving up the power lately? Could it be the inability to foresee what comes next if you let go a bit of that control to your students? Education PowerED is saying that is the level of work you need to do on your journey of becoming a culturally responsive educator.

Accordingly, once we were very clear on our positionality as educators and made the sound choice to reposition ourselves so that we are true facilitators of the learning, we took the time to elevate student voice and student choice. In all of our experiences, the students spoke about their experiences, cultural backgrounds, ways of being, and knowing within the classroom in manners that they probably could have never imagined before. There is something that we all use within our classrooms, called collective or productive struggle. The classroom environment is a space created where we can all make mistakes, including the teacher, and it is ok. As the educator, I will allow my students to struggle just a bit together, although I may know the answer because I believe that when they are close to that point of solving their problems, I will always be there to catch them. As leaders, we notice that teachers tend to cut the students' struggles short because they do not want to see the students fail or are fearful that they will give up if they struggle too much. But isn't that what life is all about? Learning to solve our problems. Having the tools and skills to persevere through adversity. We are here to say that if you build the environment that "if you try, we, as a classroom will catch you when you fall," we will not criticize you, we will not judge you, we will not place you on the outside of the classroom door isolated from your peers, we will not complain about you to other teachers, because as the educator, I know that your academic achievement is not a basis of your character, but a direct result of your learning experiences. This is when we will see student progress increase exponentially.

Furthermore, connecting the learning to the outside of the four walls of the classroom was also a common theme. Acknowledging as educators that things are

> **Student voice and student choice builds student investment.**

going on in this world today, on the outside of this school building, impacting my students on the inside of this classroom. We cannot ignore this. There are way too many classrooms that we have observed where students are not knowledgeable about how the content connects to them as a person, as a human, and their neighborhoods as a community. Unfortunately, we have seen that educators would like to leave that up to the parents. However, we challenge you to open that classroom door, not just welcome your students in or allow them to leave but open it up to the community that your students come from. Find out which are the local organizations that are assisting with healthcare and economic stability in the classroom. Find out how to provide better food choices if there is a food desert in the neighborhood.

There is one school that we know of that wanted to provide healthier food choices for their students and families and wanted to combat that food desert in the neighborhood. After surveying the students, they noticed that access to healthier food choices and grocery stores was the challenge. They also found that parents may not have had access to transportation to drive the additional ten to fifteen miles to receive better food options. Or, if the parents were new to the country or have always been in the surrounding grocery food chains, they may not have been knowledgeable about better food options. Because the school administration knew that the school was the central point where the students and the families met every day, they organized a food pantry drop-off with the local food bank that provided free access for all families to come and pick up groceries for their home and their families. Because parents were picking up the students after school, the administration would schedule the food distribution closer to school dismissal. A food truck would bring healthier food options to the school in the afternoon twice a month, and parents could receive boxes containing those alternatives. Student volunteers would be trained on how to get parents registered for the food pantry. They would be trained on how to serve the families when they arrived by letting them know about the healthier options. The students would receive community service hours for their work, and the families would walk away with better health possibilities and groceries for their households. This program would feed approximately 200–300 families per month. The students felt a sense of pride because of the impact they were making in their community. It also was a testament to combating the myth about low-income families and neighborhoods and healthier food choices. It was not that they did not want more nutritious options for themselves and their families. It was because they had no other options based on the circumstances of their environment. But it was a significant experience for both students and families.

We also must find out who are the local civic leaders that can come to the classroom to encourage the students to be a part of the civic change around them and invite our parents in and keep them informed. As educators, we know that school is hard on both our students and our parents. However, if we never open our doors for more than welcoming our students in and allowing them to leave; if we continue to simply drive to the school building, without learning about the community that surrounds it, about its history, about its changes, about its triumphs, its access and disparities. We cannot complain about our support system. We need the village.

We also hope that you can see why our students were compelled to do the work along with us beyond just complying. We showed up as our authentic selves. Our vulnerability allowed our students to be vulnerable. Our authenticity allowed our students to be authentic. There are clear boundaries that should be set between the teachers and the students in the classroom. Nonetheless, suppose we choose to have authentic conversations inside the classroom, in the hallways, or in the cafeteria, where we show a genuine interest in students' lives. In that case, we will see a shift in students' willingness to engage during classroom instruction. A step further, which we do not often hear as educators, but if we invest the time to listen to our students and empathize with our students' shared struggles, we will also see a more profound engagement into the content.

Throughout our stories, we detailed how students struggled to understand something that personally impacted them as an individual whether it had to do with societal problems or even personal challenges where they sought understanding. Even if you as an educator cannot identify with this problem because it is an experience different from yours, empathizing with the shared struggle lets students know that what is valuable to them is valuable to you. For example, if a student walks into your classroom and questions whether they should walk home because they are afraid that they will get shot by the law enforcement due to another young Black man, who looked like him, was killed and it has made national headlines. Now, as an educator, there are two choices you can make. On the one hand, you could tell the student to sit and get ready for class because that discussion has no place in the classroom. In reality, the educator should be transparent and admit that they are not equipped to talk about this topic at this magnitude.

On the other hand, the educator could ask follow-up questions. If the educator was not aware of the happening, the educator could request news articles or other reading material about the matter. The educator could seek out opportunities to learn from other colleagues and ask questions themselves. Let us be clear. We are not saying that the educator should feel sorry for the students. Empathizing with students' shared struggles requires educators to learn about worlds that may be new to them continuously.

Along these lines, we must also add that it was essential to highlight the value of student feedback in our stories. Whether it was input on students' interest for an assignment in a survey format or hearing feedback during debriefs after a meaningful learning experience, students were given opportunities to let us know, as educators, how the learning impacted them. And we listened. See, we knew that student feedback would benefit and improve the learning experiences of our students in the long term. As educators, we know that it is easier and expected to receive feedback during walkthrough evaluations or one-on-one administrative sessions with the intention that we adjust our instruction based on real-time feedback on our classroom instruction. However, how often do we take honest feedback from our students? Believe it or not, it will be one of the most beneficial tools you have in your teacher toolbox.

Lastly, we also hope that you noticed that we often used critical feedback to reflect, revise, and adjust our instruction to meet the needs of our students without overlooking the need for rigorous instruction in academic achievement (Hammond, 2015). Nevertheless, we would like for you to walk away with a clear definition of rigor. Just because you make the assignment longer than its original version does not mean it is rigorous. Just because, in your mind, you have crafted a more challenging assignment than usual does not mean that you have created a rigorous assignment for your students. We believe the disconnect with rigor in academia is when educators believe rigor directly aligns with the learning standards for the specific core content. We believe this is a minimalist understanding of the term rigor. To take it a step further, rigor means the ability to challenge students in ways that allow them to meet the expectations of the learning standards.

All in all, we recognize that genuinely embodying the characteristics of a culturally responsive educator and creating a sound, culturally responsive classroom takes some time, work, and practice. We also acknowledge that teacher disposition plays a critical role in the practice and implementation of cultural responsiveness. In essence, a teacher's disposition means an educator's natural mental and emotional outlook on the world; their attitude on a given subject. Believe it or not, our attitude influences our approach. Educators cannot effectively practice cultural responsiveness if they do not believe that every student can succeed. Educators cannot effectively practice cultural responsiveness if they do not think every student's cultural background should be entrenched in the curriculum and instruction. Educators cannot effectively practice cultural responsiveness if they are not aware of their own biases and how they may or may not impact classroom instruction and their approach to education. Educators cannot practice cultural responsiveness if they do not recognize how health, economic, and access disparities in a student's environment impacts their classroom learning ability. An educator's attitude influences the way that they shape the learning experiences of students. According to Blanchet-Cohen and Reilly (2013), a teacher's disposition can be defined by various factors.

*Challenges included value clashes, a lack of every-
day experiences, and reconciling contradictory
educational perspectives and political policies, often
placing teachers in paradoxical positions. Findings
suggest moving toward culturally responsive environmental education practices that demand more than
awareness but include interactive dialogue. Teachers
need support beyond the classroom and develop a
curriculum facilitating students' culture (pp. 12–22).*

In addressing an educators' disposition about the implementation of cultural responsiveness, we, as an educational
system, must provide the proper support; support within
the classroom, within the campus, within the district, and as
an educational network. It seems that as our conversations
about classroom inclusivity continue to shift drastically, however, the level of support for these shifts tends to dwindle. So,
where do we start?

Teacher preparation programs are designed to provide new teachers, undergraduate, and graduate students,
and alternative certification programs the tools and skills to
become licensed teachers in education. Based on the teacher's pathway, from specialized programs to foundational
components of becoming a teacher, teacher preparation programs are the place we should begin digging into the practice
of cultural responsiveness. A few programs across the country
may have modules of cultural responsiveness or specific classes designed to teach the theory. However, to truly impact

change, we must ensure that culturally responsive practice is embedded in preparing our new teachers for the classroom, from theory to practice (Irvin, 2004). There should not simply be a surface-level understanding of cultural responsiveness. We should begin thinking of cultural responsiveness as the fundamental aspect of teaching, instead of a supplemental idea that "we get to it when we get to it." Let's take a moment to think about the impact on our students of color.

According to a recent report released by The New Teacher Project, using data from the US Department of Education, there are growing concerns about the lack of diversity in teacher preparation programs. At the same time, our classrooms continue to shift in demographics. They found that teacher preparation programs are overwhelmingly whiter than the demographic makeup of the public-school population across the majority of the states in the United States. Additionally, teacher preparation programs have a compelling number of white teachers, 90%, enrolled in many programs across the country. On the other hand, alternative certification programs tend to have a more diverse demographic makeup of future teachers than most traditional teacher preparation programs (Au and Blake, 2003). If research has found that students of color tend to graduate at higher rates, are less likely to receive harsh consequences, such as suspensions, and are more likely to attend a higher level of learning institution when they encounter at least one teacher of color in their educational career than if they had none, we must begin to start thinking about if our programs that are intended to prepare future teachers to enter the classroom, where a significant number of students of color sit in those desks, then how might the experiences of our students of color be influenced? If the trend of attendees in our teacher preparation programs continues on the same pathway, then what must we do to improve the experiences of all students to ensure that they are receiving the most authentic, challenging, engaging, meaningful learning experience is to prepare them for our classrooms properly.

Not only have we provided you with true anecdotes of the practice of how we incorporated cultural responsiveness in our classrooms, but we would also like for you to consider a few recommendations within your educational institution to spark change in improving the student experiences of students of color through cultural responsiveness. These recommendations are in no way an exhaustive list of guidance for practicing cultural responsiveness. However, it is a place to start, whether through conversations, or action with your school and district leaders.

RECOMMENDATION 1

Redefine your mission and vision to encompass a culturally responsive focus.

Whether it is in your classroom or the entire school campus as a whole, you have to ensure that everyone is clear and focused on a shared vision and mission of cultural responsiveness. Even if your mission and vision are already constructed, revisiting a school or classroom's mission and vision should be a consistent practice. Your mission and vision do not have to have the exact terms "culturally responsive focus," however, redefining your mission and vision will start critical discussions around how you and your school define the term; what it means to all students and staff. How is it inclusive of every student and their community? If possible, involving a representative group to help craft your mission and vision would also be helpful. We would also recommend considering the theory and research behind cultural responsiveness. As we have stated from the beginning of our book, prominent scholars such as Dr. Gloria Ladson-Billings, Sharroky Hollie, Dr. Geneva Gay, Dr. James A. Banks, Zaretta Hammond, Dr. Christopher Emdin, and beyond have provided extensive research and understanding of how this term has evolved. One of the pitfalls of cultural responsiveness is that schools and school districts only understand the term at the surface level. Because it has become the new buzzword, often it is thought of as a checklist item, visited once every few months. However, there should be a shared commitment to understanding how cultural responsiveness can improve the experiences of students of color by ensuring that the mission and vision clarify the how, what, and who we serve.

RECOMMENDATION 2

Recruit and retain mission-driven educators, faculty, and staff and consistently train them on cultural responsiveness.

We understand the difficulty of meeting student achievement expectations mandated by the district or state, driving students toward success, as well as making sure that faculty, staff, and students are cared for during the academic school year, without even discussing the impact of the COVID-19 pandemic on education. However, once you have redefined your mission and vision to a more culturally responsive focus, a critical step is recruiting those who are mission-aligned. One aspect of recruiting is seeking ways to diversify the hiring pool to increase your chances of finding more educators who reflect your student population. We have discussed before how the lack of diversity of the teaching pool may lead to the disconnect with students of color. Because there are vast opportunity gaps in leadership pathways, pay and resources between educators of color and white educators, there has been a multitude of research reports about not only the recruitment but also retention of educators of color. Most have found that educators of color serve a critical role in shaping the school experience of students of color. Therefore, to create a culturally affirming environment, we must leverage the strengths of educators who are prepared and willing to learn how to cultivate purposeful learning experiences for all students and consistently develop teachers through professional development opportunities to serve a diverse student population. Continuous learning about the effectiveness of cultural responsiveness is critical to transforming our classrooms.

RECOMMENDATION 3

Study the practice of culturally responsive teaching that includes peer-to-peer feedback, classroom observations, and coaching cycles.

We have consistently discussed how we chose to take cultural responsiveness from theory to practice. Beyond simply reading the culturally responsive material, we must build in the practice of investing time to implement the material. One of the most effective ways to do this is to ensure that we provide opportunities for teachers to observe other teachers who are effectively practicing cultural responsiveness in their classrooms. We believe that it is one thing to learn during professional development, however, a completely different perspective is viewed when peers can walk into one another's classroom and see how the learning is impacted within the classroom environment. This is where you get to see how students are responding to culturally responsive practices and use the holistic data to learn how to adjust instruction accordingly based on the needs of the students. This is where educators can also provide peer-to-peer feedback to help one another develop as effective educators. Although schools may already do traditional coaching cycles for all teachers' lessons and academic development, using this practice specifically to analyze and evaluate cultural responsiveness using Education PowerED's culturally responsive standards could significantly impact classroom instruction.

RECOMMENDATION 4

Do the work as educators, whether it is anti-bias practice, anti-racism, or social justice awareness.

When you first hear the phrase, "do the self-work," you may immediately respond, "well, I am." You are purchasing the suitable material and resources, studying the theory of cultural responsiveness, implementing the practice, and doing everything in your power outlined in this book. Yes, you have begun the work. However, doing the self-work means that as an educator serving students of color, you need to take some time, either with a facilitator, moderators, during professional learning communities or on your own, to dive into your identity development journey.

If you did not know, there are a multitude of identity development models and frameworks for various racial and ethnic groups such as American Indian Identity Development, Asian American Identity Development, Black American Identity Development, Latino Identity Development, White Racial Identity Development,. and Biracial Identity Development just to name a few. Digging into your own racial and ethnic background will reveal aspects of yourself that you may have never known of. It is certainly not a practice to point fingers or blame others for all of the world's problems. However, it will provide a better understanding of the personal journeys our students go through every single day of their lives. We ask that all personnel in educational institutions take the time to do this because it will most certainly reveal how we are shaping our students' racial and ethnic identities when they walk into our classrooms. Think about this. From the chosen curriculum to the texts your students read, to the historical contexts you provide to build schema, to the stories that you tell within a given day in your classroom, are you affirming stories of resistance or stories of victimization? Are your norms and policies within the classroom representative of the racial and ethnic identity makeup of your student population? Do you often discuss the positive contributions of communities of color that counter stereotypes, or do you uphold them? You will only answer these questions with complete honesty and transparency if you do the self-work first.

Then your outlook should most certainly reveal your gaps of understanding, your gaps of being and knowing, your gaps in empathizing with other communities different from yours. We often respond in distinct ways because we claim we do not know or were not informed. To get to the empowering stage of your identity development model, you must do the self-work as an educator. This practice will lend itself to avowing your authenticity as an educator.

RECOMMENDATION 5

Learn from the school's local community on how to do it right.

Many times, as educators, we turn to books, and material resources, including this one, as well as professional developments from expert speakers to provide the answers we are seeking to best serve the students who are entering our classrooms. But what we should be doing is looking around at the surrounding community and environment to learn how to serve our students best. Think about it. If we understand how to serve our community best, we know how to serve our students best. The community will tell us everything that we need to know. If we immerse ourselves within the surrounding community where our schools are located, we better understand intercultural relations and connections. For example, just imagine for a bit, if we take a look inside the barbershops that have stood the test of time in every community, we can see firsthand the camaraderie, the respect, and the appreciation of the community members that frequent these places often. That one student you may have thought acts out because their mother revealed to you at a parent-teacher conference that she is a single parent. Now, in your classroom, this student may be reluctant to share out during group discussion, hesitant to read aloud, distant from his peers during collaboration, and walk around with what may seem like a chip on his shoulder every single day. You may attribute his behavior to a lack of male leadership within the home. However, you may not have known that this particular student may have four or five male figures that he checks in with every Saturday morning while he is getting his haircut. The same barbershop his family members and siblings may have attended for generations past and those to come. When he walks in, they call his name with joy and high spirit, and he speaks to every individual with a smile. He sits in the chair to get his haircut as he taps his foot to the smooth tunes on the radio, listening to lessons about life and love, how to overcome challenges, and celebrate triumphs from the surrounding conversations. The head barber begins to inquire about this student's family because he knows them all so well. The barber listens closely as he meticulously cuts the young man's hair, tailored to his liking. There is a mutual understanding between the young man and his barber, mutual respect, a form of admiration. When the student needs discipline, the barber and other male figures are there, not to scold him in front of others, not to embarrass him, not to give up on him, but to show him the way to do better; to be a better young man. When the student needs to be celebrated, the barber and other male figures are there to sing his praises to every other individual in that barbershop, whether he knows them or not. They are there as the student's confidant, his go-to, his strength when he feels like giving up. And when he exits the barber chair, they are there to witness him put on his cloak of confidence and pride. And once he leaves the barbershop, he has a renewed sense of self, purpose, and meaning. His sense of belonging is stamped within this sacred place. If you have never been into a community barbershop, I guarantee you, whichever one you step into, this is what you will see. This is the way our classrooms should invite our youth, our students of color, into our spaces and hold on to them until we have to let go. This is how we should be tailoring our curriculum and instruction to fit our students' needs instead of the other way around. Our lessons are right in front of us, from the surrounding community. When will we learn?

WORKBOOK PLANNING GUIDE

WHAT'S YOUR PLAN?

We have provided a guide for you to think through strategic plans for each domain. Take some time to collaborate with school staff and campus leaders to start the conversation around transforming your classroom environments. Remember, this is only the beginning. The goal is for you to take these plans and expound upon them to create a sound, culturally responsive classroom from theory to practice.

Community Partnerships		
School Address	City	
State	Zip Code	
Community Demographics		
Local Organizations		
Local Representatives		
Area Access *(Healthcare, Grocery Stores, Transportation, Education, Communication, Economics, Resources)*		
What percentage of your students are from the surrounding community?		
Distinctive Strengths and Challenges of Community		
Who will be responsible for community outreach and partnerships? How will it be impactful to your classroom?	Start Date/Time Commitment	
How will you support students and build relationships with them outside of the classroom setting?		

Culture Management	
How will you create opportunities for your students to get to know you to build trust within the classroom?	
Teacher to Students	Students to Teacher
What values, beliefs, and mindsets do you want the classroom community to embody?	
In what ways will students have the ability to give input and help shape classroom systems, routines, and other functions? List them below and define how you expect students to provide input.	
System/Routine	Student Input
How do you plan to learn about your students' interests, identities, and cultural backgrounds?	
How will you consistently refuel and maintain your high energy despite challenges that may come up in the academic school year?	
What mediums will you use to ignite student investment?	
Call & Response	Music
Media	Technology

Authentic Engagement	
Overall Lesson Goals	
What is your class-wide academic goal?	How does this goal differ from the previous years' goal?
How will students determine their individual growth and achievement goals this year?	
Planning for Authentic Engagement	
Lesson Standard	
Lesson Objective	
What real-world purpose does your content serve to students in their long-term futures?	
Connection to Current Events	Connection to Past Events

Authentic Engagement	
How are your content, lesson strategies, and activities uniquely positioned to encourage students' identity & leadership development?	
How will you allow students to provide evaluative feedback on the lesson? How will you adjust your instruction based on the feedback?	
Survey Format	Whole Group Share Out
Focus Groups	Anonymous Submissions

Social Justice Curriculum	
Social Justice Topic:	Connection to Learning Objectives:
My implicit and explicit bias that may potentially advance the learning on the topic?	
My implicit and explicit bias that may potentially hinder the learning on the topic?	
Desired Outcome for Students after Exploration of Topic *(Civic Engagement, Community Service, Self-Actualization, etc.)*	
How will this topic help build students' self-concept and agency?	
Is there an immediate or distant impact on the surrounding community, students' identity, and/or cultural background?	
Historical Context of Topic	
In what ways and/or formats will student voice be elevated?	
Oral Presentations	Peer-to-Peer Discussion (Large or Small)
Written Form	Social Media Campaign
Additional staff/support needed	

REFERENCES

Au, K. H., & Blake, K. M. (2003). Cultural identity and learning to teach in a diverse community: Findings from a collective case study. *Journal of Teacher Education*, 54(3), 192–205.

Aguado, T., Ballesteros, B., & Malik, B. (2003). Cultural diversity and school equity. A model to evaluate and develop educational practices in multicultural education contexts. *Equity & Excellence in Education*, *36*(1), 50–63.

Banks, J. A., & McGee, B. C. A. (2004). *Handbook of research on multicultural education*. Jossey-Bass.

Banks, J. A. (2007). *Educating citizens in a multicultural society*. Teachers College Press.

Banks, J. A., & McGee, B. C. A. (2020). *Multicultural education: Issues and perspectives*. John Wiley & Sons.

Bazzaz, D. (2017). *School stats: Racial achievement gaps exist even in Washington's highest-performing schools*. The Seattle Times. Available from https://www.seattletimes.com/education-lab/school-stats-racial-achievement-gaps-exist-even-in-states-highest-performing-schools/ (Accessed: 19 September 2021).

Blanchet-Cohen, N., & Reilly, R. C. (2013). Teachers' perspectives on environmental education in multicultural contexts: Towards culturally-responsive environmental education. *Teaching and Teacher Education*, *36*, 12–22.

Darling-Hammond, L. (2017). Teaching for social justice: Resources, relationships, and anti-racist practice. *Multicultural Perspectives*, *19*(3), 133–138.

Emdin, C. (2017). *For white folks who teach in the hood . . . and the rest of y'all too: Reality pedagogy and Urban Education*. Beacon Press.

Fay, L. (2018). *The State of America's student-teacher racial gap: Our public school system has been majority-minority for years, but 80 percent of teachers are still white*. Available from https://www.the74million.org/article/the-state-of-americas-student-teacher-racial-gap-our-public-school-system-has-been-majority-minority-for-years-but-80-percent-of-teachers-are-still-white/ (Accessed: 19 September 2021).

García, E. E. (2008). *Teaching and learning in two languages: Bilingualism & Schooling in the United States*. Teachers College Press.

Gregson, S. A. (2013). Negotiating social justice teaching: One full-time teacher's practice viewed from the trenches. *Journal for Research in Mathematics Education*, *44*(1), 164–198.

Hammond, Z. L. (2015). *Culturally responsive teaching and the brain: Promoting authentic engagement and rigor among culturally and linguistically diverse students*. Corwin Press.

Irvine, J. J. (1991). *Black students and school failure: Policies, practices, and prescriptions*. Praeger.

Irvine, J. J. (2004). *Educating teachers for diversity: Seeing with a cultural eye*. Teachers College Press.

Kaplan, E. (2019). Want mastery? Let students find their own way. Edutopia – How to promote mastery-based learning, edutopia. Available from: http://www.edutopia.org/article/want-mastery-let-students-find-their-own-way (Accessed 11 December 2021).

Ladson-Billings, G. (2009). *The dreamkeepers: Successful teachers of African American children, 2nd ed*. John Wiley & Sons.

McGee, B. C. A. (2005). *Improving multicultural education: Lessons from the Intergroup Education Movement*. Teachers College Press.

McKinley, J. (2010). *Raising black students' achievement through culturally responsive teaching*. ASCD.

Ochoa, G. L., & Pineda, D. (2008). Deconstructing power, privilege, and silence in the classroom. *Radical History Review*, *2008*(102), 45–62.

Parker, W. (2003). *Teaching democracy: Unity and diversity in public life*. Teacher's College Press.

Pedaste, M., Mäeots, M., Siiman, L. A., Jong, T., van Riesen, S. A. N., Kamp, E. T., Manoli, C. C., Zacharia, Z. C., & Tsourlidaki, E. (2015). Phases of inquiry-based learning: Definitions and the inquiry cycle. *Educational Research Review*, 14, 47–61.

Ready, T., Edley, C. F., & Snow, C. E. (2002). *Achieving high educational standards for all conference summary*. National Academy Press.

Revell, M. D. (2021). Sustaining culturally responsive teaching practices. *Research Anthology on Culturally Responsive Teaching and Learning*, 499–520.

Schmid, S., & Bogner, F. X. (2015). Effects of students' effort scores in a STRUCTURED inquiry unit on LONG-TERM recall abilities of content knowledge. *Education Research International*, 2015, 1–11, doi:10.1155/2015/826734.

Seider, S., Graves, D., El-Amin, A., Soutter, M., Tamerat, J., Jennett, P., Clark, S., Malhotra, S., & Johannsen, J. (2017). Developing sociopolitical consciousness of race and social class inequality in adolescents attending progressive and no excuses urban secondary schools. *Applied Developmental Science*, *22*(3), 169–187.

Wall, V. A. (2018). It's time to plant hope. In K. L. Guthrie & V. S. Chunnoo (Eds), Changing the narrative: Socially just leadership education (pp. xi – xiii) [Foreward] Charlotte, NC: Information Age Publishing

APPENDIX A: 7 POWER ELEMENTS

For extended practice, we would like to note that during our research in developing the culturally responsive standards, we found seven emergent themes that span all domains. These themes, referred to as Power Elements, are student-centered learning theories that inform a culturally responsive educator's beliefs and behaviors throughout the practice and implementation of cultural responsiveness. This list is as follows: essential skill development, leadership development, racial identity development, restorative justice, social-emotional learning, sociopolitical consciousness, and student experience.

Educators more commonly recognize the power elements as individual practices or suggestive approaches to better support students. We have found that staff professional development often features one-time workshops or teaching cultural responsiveness components in isolation, which is ineffective at producing lasting change within the classroom environment. Therefore, in addition to being immersed in the theory and practice of cultural responsiveness, educators must be engaged in the learning that emphasizes how these power elements work in concert to foster a culturally responsive classroom environment.

We believe that proficiency in one element is directly correlated to proficiency in the other aspects. Therefore, educators must understand the core principles and practices underlying each power element in relation to one another. They should be regarded as prerequisite knowledge for educators to become proficient in implementing relevant Culturally Responsive Teaching standards into their practice. We have created a distinct symbol that has been adopted to represent each Power Element, as demonstrated in the table below and have also provided a guided reference to how the elements are embedded within the Culturally Responsive Domains and Standards. On completion of this book, we hope that you have the knowledge and skills to create transformative change inside your classroom.

Power Element	Description	Symbol
Essential Skill Development	Culturally Responsive Educators recognize that students who experience racism, classism, and oppression will need additional tools to overcome marginalization. Classrooms should provide opportunities for students to practice and master the essential skills required to become facilitators of social change.	
Experiential Learning	Culturally Responsive Educators design classroom experiences that maintain lasting connection with learning, increase student motivation, and impact emotion on learning. Classrooms should allow students to critically reflect on their learning experience.	

Leadership Development	Culturally Responsive Educators equip students with the experiences needed to become a valuable resource in their schools, their communities, and future occupations. Classrooms should provide opportunities for students to problem-solve, engage in decision-making, and serve as role models.	
Identity Development	Culturally Responsive Educators understand that exposing students to curriculum that resembles their racial backgrounds leads to higher levels of entitlement, ownership, and confidence in the classroom. Classrooms should make space for students to talk about the diverse experiences of others, especially people of color.	
Restorative Justice	Culturally Responsive Educators utilize non-punitive, relationship-centered approaches for avoiding and addressing harm, responding to violations of culture norms and collaboratively solving problems. Classrooms should allow students to engage in accountability and leverage misbehavior as moments for learning.	

Social Emotional Learning	Culturally Responsive Educators support students in acknowledging, addressing, and healing from the ways we have been impacted by racism and systemic oppression. Classrooms should foster inclusive, liberatory learning environments to give students a sense of belonging, agency to shape the content and process of their learning and thrive.	
Sociopolitical Consciousness	Culturally Responsive Educators help students critically analyze the political, economic, and social forces shaping society and their status in it. Classrooms should aid in building students' resilience and civic engagement.	

APPENDIX B: REFERENCE GUIDE

CULTURALLY RESPONSIVE TEACHING STANDARDS AND DOMAINS + POWER ELEMENTS

This appendix links the domains mentioned in the book's introduction with the 7 Power Elements listed above. It is meant to serve as a reminder that all culturally responsive educators must be well-rounded in their practice to create an optimal environment for all.

Domain 1: Community Partnerships

Standard	Title	Description "The Culturally Responsive Teacher is able to. . ."	Power Element
1.1	Community Knowledge	Gain critical knowledge about the local community and students' families, including history, culture and values. Teacher leverages community knowledge to foster a safe and responsive learning environment.	

1.2	Family Involvement	Develop trusting relationships with diverse families to maintain involvement throughout the year. Teacher consistently incorporates family input and insight when determining academic goals, curriculum, and expectations.	
1.3	Contextual Learning	Build bridges of meaning between the classroom and the student's home community. Teacher utilizes real-world events, issues, and information as the basis by which students explore and engage in learning.	
1.4	Support Systems	Invites family and community members to be active participants in maintaining the social emotional well-being of students. Teacher facilitates opportunities for students to talk about identity, experiences, and other aspects of their lives.	

1.5	Local Partnerships	Partners with local organizations, businesses, and leaders to maximize learning experiences through guest presentations, interviews, demonstrations, etc.	
1.6	Community Service	Create opportunities for students to build community through volunteerism that directly benefits the community.	

Domain 2: Culture Management

Standard	Title	Description **"The Culturally Responsive Teacher is able to. . ."**	Power Element
2.1	High Expectations	Explicitly communicate high expectations for students academically and socially. The teacher ensures expectations are reflective of students' home culture and identity.	

2.2	Collective Responsibility	Create a community-centered learning environment where students are expected to be individually and collectively accountable for successes and failures. Teacher structures environments for cooperative learning and group activities.	
2.3	Relationships	Establish meaningful interpersonal relationships with all students and foster healthy interactions between students. Teacher-student relationships extend beyond the bounds of the classroom as the teacher shows genuine interest in each student.	
2.4	Authenticity	Celebrate the social, cultural, and linguistic differences among students openly and explore these differences with students. The teacher encourages students to represent themselves authentically (verbal communication, body language, cultural expressions, etc.)	

2.5	Harmony	Nurture positive emotions in students that will support learning and ensure that students feel safe, cared for, and welcomed. The teacher supports students in developing a positive self-image and beliefs about others.	
2.6	Organization of Space	Establish a physically inviting classroom where decor, posters, flags, and other educational materials featured throughout the classroom reflect the cultural diversity of the students and the school community. The teacher arranges classroom space optimally for social interactions including small group discussions, presentations, movement, and teacher-student collaborative space.	
2.7	Classroom Systems	Cultivates a classroom environment that reflects diversity, equity, and justice. Teacher actions apply equitably to all students while ensuring policies, procedures, and rewards do not isolate certain groups of students.	

| 2.8 | Student-Led Management | Involves students in democratic decision making around expectations, discipline, and policies that impact the learning environment. The teacher leverages students to critique and shape all classroom systems. | |

Domain 3: Authentic Engagement

Standard	Title	Description **"The Culturally Responsive Teacher is able to. . ."**	Power Element
3.1	Meaningful Experiences	Plan purposeful experiences that allow students to role play, problem solve, and interact with one another in unique ways. Teacher designs activities that encourage students to create multicultural songs, dances, performances, and presentations.	

3.2	Lesson Structure	Apply various instructional strategies (teacher-centered presentations, discussions, demonstrations, activities, etc.) to facilitate students' learning. Teacher carefully drafts activities to complement student thinking.	
3.3	Differentiation & Rigor	Scaffold the learning from basic to higher order thinking to activate prior knowledge, connect with students of various learning preferences, and support all students to produce high-quality work and solve complex issues.	
3.4	Inquiry-Based Learning	Facilitate learning processes that position students as drivers of their own learning and provide multiple ways for students to question and interpret the content they are learning.	

3.5	Energy & Pace	Utilize their bodies, voices, and facial gestures as teaching instruments to maintain a brisk pace. Teacher models a positive attitude and frequently embeds elements of playfulness and competition into the learning.	
3.6	Collaboration	Design learning that creates interdependent relationships amongst students. Teacher structures groups in familiar and unfamiliar ways to ensure that students share important roles and have opportunities to develop expertise.	
3.7	Student Discourse	Emphasize teacher-student dialogue through whole group, small group, and peer conversations (discussion, debate, storytelling, reflection, etc.)	

3.8	Shared Evaluation	Provide students with the opportunity to evaluate the effectiveness of the lessons as well as determine unique, creative ways to evaluate their academic performance. Learning is assessed by a variety of measures.	
3.9	Physical Movement	Implement active engagement strategies to keep students physically and psychologically involved. Teacher uses physical activities to stimulate learning or interest.	
3.10	Multimedia & Technology	Complement the traditional curriculum with multimedia (examples, newspaper clippings, articles, song lyrics, plays, comics, video games, images, etc.) to spark student interest and curiosity. Teacher provides opportunities for students to utilize technology as a medium to facilitate and demonstrate learning.	

Domain 4: Social Justice

Standard	Title	Description **"The Culturally Responsive Teacher is able to. . ."**	Power Element
4.1	Self-Concept	Reinforce positive attributes of students' identity and focus on students' values, feelings, and beliefs about themselves. Teacher engages in discussion about how self-concept is influenced by students' sociopolitical context (Individual, Collective, Institutional, and Ideological).	
4.2	Understanding of Inequity	Equip students with knowledge and understanding of the history of inequality and oppression. Teacher helps students recognize inequity as a result of human-created social and economic relations that can be challenged.	
4.3	Cultural Knowledge	Select curriculum materials where students explore a variety of cultures and groups through artifacts, history, etc. Students gain an authentic knowledge of different ethnic groups and an appreciation of diversity.	

4.4	Content Relevance	Provide curriculum materials on social, economic, and political issues related to ethnicity, gender, and exceptionality. Teacher plans learning encounters that validate students' lived realities, cultural identities, and heritage.	
4.5	Anti-Bias Themes	Structure learning to allow for deep exploration of anti-bias themes. Teacher models how to identify, interpret, and speak out against bias.	
4.6	Diverse Perspectives	Use curriculum materials that describe historical, social, and political events from a wide range of racial, ethnic, cultural, and language perspectives. Teacher encourages students to develop multicultural perspectives that respect the dignity and worth of all people.	
4.7	Social Action	Construct scenarios for students to practice social advocacy skills and utilize tools of activism to become effective change agents in the school and broader community.	

		Teacher assigns activities that challenge students to examine their beliefs and engage in the struggle to make society more equitable.	
4.8	Agency	Encourage students to analyze the circumstances of their lived experiences and develop practical tools to persevere through challenges stemming from social injustice.	

ABOUT THE AUTHORS

DAVID MCDONALD, M.ED.

A native of Dallas, Texas, David McDonald has been recognized as an awarded educator, unapologetic community advocate, and an impactful social entrepreneur. He graduated from The University of Texas at Austin with dual degrees in Applied Learning & Development and African & African American Studies. He received his Master of Education in Teaching & Learning from Southern Methodist University, specializing in Gifted & Talented Instruction for culturally diverse learners. He is now the Founder and managing partner of Education PowerED and leverages his influence across organizations such as the NAACP, National Urban League, Black Chamber of Commerce, and more.

His accomplishments have continued throughout his career as he was later recognized by the Desoto ISD Board of Trustees and Horace Mann for his teaching excellence. David has been featured in Aljazeera, *Los Angeles Times*, *The Daily Texan*, University Business, *USA Today*, and many local publications. David has led leadership sessions across various industries, ranging in size from 5 to 1,000. He helps them to find a deeper purpose, achieve better collaboration, and increase their impact overall. His high-energy keynote presentations make him a top-rated speaker at every event.

At his core, David is a servant leader. He has used his influence to advocate for policies centered on equity and secured over $120,000 to support the education of underrepresented students. He has been recognized for his efforts to improve the quality of education in the city of Dallas by supporting initiatives such as Dallas Kids First, Stand for Children, and Minority Student Recruitment at UT Austin.

DANIELLE ROSS, M.ED.

Danielle Ross is originally from Houston, Texas, with roots in Memphis, Tennessee, and serves as the Co-Founder and Partner of Education PowerED. She graduated from the University of Texas at Austin with a Bachelor of Science in Communication Studies and a Master of Education from Southern Methodist University with a concentration in Gifted and Talented Curriculum & Instruction. Danielle's style of pedagogy emphasizes the importance of cultural relevancy and authentic student engagement in the classroom. She has a unique way of bringing all student perspectives to the forefront of learning to engage and highlight student voice during instruction. She co-founded a social enterprise, Education PowerED, with the mission to generate culturally responsive solutions and resources to end educational inequity for students of color.

ANDRE ROSS, M.ED.

A native of Gary, Indiana, Andre received a Bachelor of Science in Business with a concentration in Management from New York University. His experiences there compelled him to pursue a career in education to help diminish the ways in which identity markers impact educational and career trajectories. Andre served as an 8th Grade Mathematics Teacher at The Dr. Billy Earl Dade Middle School in South Dallas. Following his first year as an educator, Andre was recognized as "Teacher of the Year." In addition, Andre has increased his students' academic growth by double-digit gains during each year that he served. In June 2018, Andre accepted a role with Teach For America where he serves as Manager, Teacher Leadership Development. Andre is a Co-founder and Chief Curriculum Officer with the Education PowerED family.

SHONTORIA WALKER, ED.D.

Dr. Shontoria Walker is a graduate from the University of Houston in Houston, Texas, with a degree in Professional Leadership with an emphasis in Literacy. Her research focuses on using culturally relevant pedagogy to influence literacy achievement for Middle School Black Male Students based on her experiences as a former 8th grade English teacher at an all-boys preparatory academy. She has also served on the Texas Teacher Advisory Board, a Teach Plus Policy Fellow as well as a Senior Policy Fellow with Teach Plus Texas from 2014–2019. During her time and beyond she has advocated for educational policy laws that directly impacted the classroom as well as contributed to policy briefings for the revision of *The Every Student Succeeds Act* and national policy reports such as *If You Listen, We Will Stay: Why Teachers of Color Leave and How To Disrupt*

Teacher Turnover and *To Be Who We Are: Black Teachers on Creating Affirming School Cultures*.

She currently serves as the Executive Director and Partner of Education PowerED. In her everyday work she is committed to collaborating with teachers, administrators, and district leaders to ensure that all students receive an equitable literacy education across the district. Graduating with distinction as summa cum laude of her doctorate cohort, her passion and dedication to literacy education and equitable educational policy laws is interminable.

ACKNOWLEDGMENTS

We would like to acknowledge and thank the renowned scholars, those who have pioneered the culturally responsive teaching journey, for defining spaces for students and educators like us to thrive

To Christ Temple Church (Gary, IN), thank you for all of the memorable, rich experiences I had there as a child. They have shaped me personally and professionally.

—Andre

INDEX